MW00627115

Envirc

Nathan J. Clark
Environmental Financial Products, LLC

Murali Kanakasabai
Environmental Financial Products, LLC

Rafael L. Marques
Environmental Financial Products, LLC

Environmental Markets: A New Asset Class

CFA Institute
Research
Foundation

Statement of Purpose

The CFA Institute Research Foundation is a not-for-profit organization established to promote the development and dissemination of relevant research for investment practitioners worldwide.

Editorial Staff

Elizabeth Collins
Book Editor

Mary-Kate Hines
Assistant Editor

Cindy Maisannes
Manager, Publications Production

Christina Hampton
Publishing Technology Specialist

Biographies

Richard L. Sandor is CEO at Environmental Financial Products, LLC (EFP), which specializes in inventing, designing, and developing new financial markets. He was honored by the city of Chicago for his recognition as the "father of financial futures." In 2007, Dr. Sandor was honored as one of *TIME* magazine's "Heroes of the Environment" for his work as the "Father of Carbon Trading." In July 2013, he was named a Chevalier in the French Legion of Honour. Dr. Sandor is a lecturer in law and economics at the University of Chicago Law School, a visiting fellow with the Smith School at the University of Oxford, and a Distinguished Professor of Environmental Finance at Guanghua School of Management at Peking University. He is the author of *Good Derivatives: A Story of Financial and Environmental Innovation.* Dr. Sandor is a senior fellow at the Milken Institute and a board member of the Clean Energy Trust and is on the advisory board for the Smithsonian Tropical Research Institute and the Center for Financial Stability. He received his bachelor of arts degree from the City University of New York, Brooklyn College, and earned his PhD in economics from the University of Minnesota. Dr. Sandor is the recipient of an honorary degree of doctor of science from the Swiss Federal Institute of Technology.

Nathan J. Clark is managing director at EFP. Prior to his work at EFP, he was senior vice president and managing director of offset programs for the Chicago Climate Exchange (CCX). In that capacity, Mr. Clark managed the process of defining and implementing project-based emission-reduction initiatives.

Murali Kanakasabai is managing director at EFP, where he leads design and implementation efforts for environmental markets and guides investment strategy for clean energy projects investments. He has more than a decade of academic and private sector experience researching climate change issues and helping design and launch several environmental markets, including the CCX. At the CCX, Dr. Kanakasabai served as senior vice president in the research department and contributed to the development of several of the world's first derivative instruments for hedging environmental risks and promoting sustainable development. He was also extensively involved in building environmental market design and market readiness around the world. Dr. Kanakasabai was senior member of the CCX Carbon Offsets team and led its international offsets portfolio. He holds a master's degree in extension education and rural sociology from the Indian Agricultural Research Institute in New Delhi and a master's degree in economics and a PhD in agricultural economics from the University of Kentucky.

Rafael L. Marques is a managing director at EFP. He previously served as senior vice president of the CCX, where he was actively involved in all phases of its development and launch. He was involved in the development and implementation of CCX international activities and joint ventures. Mr. Marques has been a delegate and presenter to several Conferences of the Parties to the United Nations Framework Convention on Climate Change. He has lectured on the subject of market-based solutions to environmental problems in the United States, Brazil, India, and China. He co-authored articles on the CCX published by the United Nations Conference on Trade and Development and by Great Britain's Royal Society. Mr. Marques holds a bachelor of arts degree from Luther College and a master's degree in economics from the University of Illinois at Chicago.

Acknowledgments

We would like to thank the following individuals who provided valuable comments, suggestions, and criticisms for this book: Alexander Barkawi, Don Blackmore, Bruce Braine, John Briscoe, Sylvie Bouriaux, Henry Derwent, Brad Georges, John Langford, Tauni Lanier, Tom Libassi, Mike MacGregor, Stephen McComb, Brian McLean, Jeff O'Hara, Brian Richter, Dan Scarbrough, Eric Taub, and William Welch. In addition to being world-class experts in their respective fields, they were incredibly generous with their time, and they worked with tight deadlines but always gave us high-level feedback and insights. Any improvements to this book should be credited to them, and any errors or omissions are certainly ours.

A special thank-you goes to our colleague Fang-Yu Liang. She diligently and tirelessly performed the tasks of researching, editing, and organizing the many versions of the manuscript while providing a fresh and critical read of the chapters. Important research assistance was also given by Yanjie Liu, Defne Ozaltun, and Karen Peterson. Our gratitude goes to all of them.

Laurence B. Siegel first approached us to write an introduction to the emerging field of environmental finance. We are very grateful to Larry and to Bud Haslett of the CFA Institute Research Foundation. They have been constant supporters of this project and also provided great suggestions and editorial work.

Richard Sandor is grateful to his wife, Ellen, and his daughters, Julie and Penya, for their suggestions and unwavering support.

We gratefully acknowledge the financial support from the CFA Institute Research Foundation for the preparation of this book.

Contents

CE Qualified Activity   **CFA Institute**   This publication qualifies for 5 CE credits under the guidelines of the CFA Institute Continuing Education Program.

Foreword

The CFA Institute Research Foundation is to be commended for sponsoring—and environmental market pioneer Richard Sandor and his three colleagues for writing—this masterly and path-finding overview of an asset class that is already important, rapidly gaining further scale and scope, and yet surprisingly and systematically underused.

My 1999 book *Natural Capitalism*, co-authored with Paul Hawken and L. Hunter Lovins, asked the question, If capitalism is the productive use of and reinvestment of capital, what is capital?[i] Industrial capitalism deals seriously with only two kinds of capital—financial capital and physical capital (i.e., money and goods). It ignores and even liquidates two still more valuable kinds of capital—natural capital and human capital (i.e., nature and people). Without people, there is no economy, and without nature, there are no people, so this omission is material. But if you play with a full deck, productively using and investing in *all four* forms of capital, then you make more money, do more good, have more fun, and gain stunning competitive advantage. The authors of this book provide here a vital toolkit for starting to capture these opportunities by valuing and investing in the salient missing parts.

Familiar environmental markets already monetize and trade in the abatement of negative environmental externalities—unpriced costs to health, wealth, and security imposed by one party on another.[ii] Avoiding these costs can be valuable: Air pollution has already cost a half-billion northern Chinese people an estimated 2.5 billion person-years of life expectancy—five years per person.[iii]

Less familiar and less mature but even more promising than improving air quality are ways to make markets in *saved resources*.[iv] Resource efficiency is typically profitable simply because (1) saving resources costs less than buying them and (2) with new integrative design techniques, efficiency often

[i]P.G. Hawken, A.B. Lovins, and L.H. Lovins, *Natural Capitalism: Creating the Next Industrial Revolution* (Boston: Little Brown, 1999); free download (with a summary of the article from the *Harvard Business Review*) at www.natcap.org.

[ii]Hank Patton has devised a transactional framework for intergenerational commerce so that people not yet born can invest today in providing the goods and services—and avoiding the "bads" and nuisances—that will advance their interests and our own; see www.worldsteward.org.

[iii]Y. Chen, A. Ebenstein, M. Greenstone, and Hongbin Li, "Evidence on the Impact of Sustained Exposure to Air Pollution on Life Expectancy from China's Huai River Policy," *Proceedings of the National Academy of Sciences* (8 July 2013): www.pnas.org/content/early/2013/07/03/1300018110.

[iv]A.B. Lovins, "Making Markets in Saved Resources" in *Festschrift for E.U. von Weizsäcker*, RMI Publication #E89-2725 (June 1989): www.rmi.org/Knowledge-Center/Library/2013-19_MakingMarketsinResourceEfficiency.

produces expanding rather than diminishing returns.[v] The savings can be dramatic: A detailed 2011 book showed how the United States, for example, could run a 2.6-fold bigger 2050 economy with no oil, coal, or nuclear energy and one-third as much natural gas—$5 trillion cheaper in net present value than "business as usual" (with all externalities valued at zero).[vi] This tripling of end-use energy efficiency and shifting of energy supplies from one-tenth to three-fourths renewable would strengthen national security, would require no new inventions or acts of Congress, and could be led by business for profit.

Yet, that study's astonishing financial returns (e.g., tripling or quadrupling US buildings' energy productivity with a 33% internal rate of return and doubling that of industry with a 21% IRR) reflect only private internal costs and benefits. Those results leave out all avoided environmental, security, and other negative externalities (including the avoidance of 82%–86% of fossil carbon emissions). They also omit major positive externalities, such as side benefits that have been well documented to transform real estate by adding value often worth one and sometimes two *orders of magnitude* more than the energy savings themselves.[vii]

The markets already being made in saved resources, so that all ways to provide or save resources can compete fairly, are impressive and valuable. But they barely scratch the surface of the asset- and wealth-creating opportunities. For example, Chapter 13 of *Natural Capitalism* outlines some of the roughly 20 new ways my team devised in the 1980s for making markets in saved energy, water, and materials.[viii] Many of these methods are gradually entering use. For example, electric grids in about three-fifths of the United States now let "negawatts" (saved electricity) and demand response (changing the timing of electrical demand) compete in formerly supply-side-only auctions. In the giant PJM power pool, 94% of the winning bids in a recent auction came from the demand side because negawatts cost less than megawatts.

In transport, some jurisdictions are starting to make markets in "negatrips" and "negamiles," encouraging competition between different ways of getting around or of not needing to. Such markets can even reward real estate

[v]A.B. Lovins, "Integrative Design: A Disruptive Source of Expanding Returns to Investments in Energy Efficiency," RMI Publication #X10-09 (2010): www.rmi.org/rmi/Library/2010-09_IntegrativeDesign; A.B. Lovins, M. Bendewald, M. Kinsley, H. Hutchinson, A. Pradhan, I. Sheikh, and Z. Acher, "Factor Ten Engineering Design Principles," RMI Publication #X10-10 (2010): www.rmi.org/rmi/Library/2010-10_10xEPrinciples.

[vi]A.B. Lovins and Rocky Mountain Institute, *Reinventing Fire: Bold Business Solutions for the New Energy Era* (White River Junction, VT: Chelsea Green, 2011): www.rmi.org/reinventingfire.

[vii]S. Muldavin, "Value beyond Energy Cost Savings" (www.greenbuildingfc.com).

[viii]This discussion is also provided in Chapter 5.3 of the predecessor to Hawken et al., *Natural Capitalism*, op cit.—namely, A.B. Lovins, E.U. von Weizsäcker, and L.H. Lovins, *Factor Four: Doubling Wealth, Halving Resource Use* (London: Earthscan, 1987):164–176.

developers. "Smart-growth" or "new-urbanist" models create or restore compact, walkable, mixed-use cities and towns that help people be already where they want to be so they need not go somewhere else. Because such layouts are more desirable and valuable, they generally boost developers' profits.

In water, efficient use is starting to bid against increased supply, and the same is true for some other resources.

These markets can spur "solutions-economy business models," which typically lease the desired service rather than selling a product whose use produces the service. Solutions-economy business models align providers' interests with customers' interests—that is, rewarding both for doing more and better with less for longer.[ix]

Underlying environmental markets are the vital principles of financial economics—sound but often dangerously overlooked. For example, the lower financial risk of the small, fast, modular investments now taking over the electricity market is one of the reasons these projects are often worth an order of magnitude more than is normally assumed.[x] Some traditional suppliers of capital continue to chase big, slow, lumpy projects. For example, huge investments are still being made on the basis of apparently low spot prices for fracked natural gas that reflect neither the attendant risks and uncertainties nor the value of the gas's price volatility. (The volatility is discoverable from the straddle in the options market and is likely to rise if the apparent cheapness of wellhead gas causes expanded exports of liquefied natural gas, petrochemical producers' pivots to cheaper gas, and downstream bottlenecking.) Counting price volatility alone approximately doubles the price of gas that is relevant for fair comparison with its constant-price carbon-free physical hedges—energy efficiency and renewables—that are increasingly outpacing and outcompeting it. Financial analysts have a duty to warn investors who ignore volatility—which is akin to constructing a bond portfolio of all junk bonds and no US Treasury bonds by considering yield but not risk. Analysts could also advise investors to short the portfolios of those who persist in such foolishness.

In addition to such tactical openings, the strategic horizon for applying financial economics and making environmental markets stretches boundlessly. Herman Daly, ecological economist and professor at the School of Public Policy at the University of Maryland, neatly summarizes how the first Industrial Revolution made people about 100 times more productive because the relative scarcity of people was limiting the exploitation of seemingly boundless nature. Today, we have the opposite pattern: abundant

---

[ix]See Hawken et al., *Natural Capitalism*, op cit., Ch. 7.

[x]A.B. Lovins, E.K. Datta, T. Feiler, K.R. Rabago, J.N. Swisher, A. Lehmann, and K. Wicker, *Small Is Profitable: The Hidden Economic Benefits of Making Electrical Resources the Right Size* (Snowmass, CO: Rocky Mountain Institute, 2002): www.smallisprofitable.org.

people but scarce nature. So, it is no longer people that we must strive to use far more productively, but nature. The four interlinked principles of natural capitalism—(1) radical resource productivity; (2) producing in the same way nature does (closed loops, no waste, no toxicity); (3) rewarding these shifts through solutions-economy business models; and (4) investing some of the resulting profits back into the kinds of capital in shortest supply (natural and human capital)—can, together, create an extraordinarily less risky, more durable, and more rewarding economy—for all, for ever.

In today's dirty, depleted, and dangerous world, environmental markets are the key both to short-term tactical opportunities and to longer-term transformational ones. I applaud Richard Sandor, Nathan Clark, Murali Kanakasabai, and Rafael Marques for crisply describing where to find the key and how to insert and turn it—and for giving us a glimpse of the treasures behind that golden door.

Amory B. Lovins
Cofounder and Chief Scientist, Rocky Mountain Institute
Old Snowmass, Colorado
2 December 2013

Preface

Forty percent of deaths worldwide are the result of environmental factors, including the secondary effects environmental degradation has in promoting disease.[xi] No corporation, government, or population is untouched by this issue. The role of markets, however, in reducing pollution and environmental degradation is not widely understood. Markets, when designed properly, can be a powerful agent for social and environmental transformation. In the United States alone, environmental markets have saved hundreds of thousands of lives and generated hundreds of billions of dollars in human health benefits.[xii] In addition to saving lives, these markets also act as economic drivers, generating jobs and improving the overall quality of life while acting as catalysts for innovation.

Population growth, industrialization, and urbanization in the past 200 years have resulted in local, national, and global pollution of our environment. Fossil-fuel combustion has resulted in overaccumulation of pollutants that cause smog, acid rain, and climate changes. Entire populations—including China, India, Africa, and large areas elsewhere—face inadequate access to clean air and water.

The lack of ownership of these precious commodities is the cause of the problem. The profit maximization model for a firm takes into account only the direct costs incurred by the firm, not the spillover costs, such as the negative repercussions associated with the pollution of air and water. Therefore, more goods and services are produced than would be if pollution were either controlled by fiat or internally priced (a condition in which the social or external cost of the pollution is figured into the decision about how much of the good or service to produce).[xiii]

These spillover costs, called "negative externalities," can be dealt with by mandating limits on emissions or requiring specific modifications in the production of goods and services. Spillover costs or benefits can also be mitigated by taxes and/or subsidies. In addition, externalities can be mitigated when public or private entities create a limited number of emission or use

---

[xi]"Pollution Causes 40% of Deaths Worldwide, Study Finds," *ScienceDaily* (14 August 2007).

[xii]Douglas A. Burns, Jason A. Lynch, Bernard J. Cosby, Mark E. Fenn, and Jill S. Baron, "An Integrated Assessment," National Acid Precipitation Assessment Program Report to Congress, US EPA Clean Air Markets Division (2011).

[xiii]An easy way to understand this statement is as follows: The external (e.g., pollution) cost of a good is added to the internal, or ordinary, cost to arrive at the total, or social, cost. If the external cost is a positive number, this process makes the good more expensive. All other things being equal, if a good becomes more expensive, then the quantity demanded is lower, so the "right" amount to produce is also lower.

rights—that is, by a cap. These property rights, called "allowances," can be purchased by companies for the purpose of compliance with environmental laws if they exceed the cap. Similarly, companies that reduce emissions in excess of their targeted reductions can sell their allowances, thereby motivating compliance at the least cost.

The creation of a limited number (cap) of property rights and their transferability (trade) has come to be known as "cap-and-trade." The transferability of allowances results in the market putting a price on the right to pollute. If that price is higher than that of the technology required to reduce or eliminate the pollution, companies will install the technology. If the opposite is the case, they will buy allowances. The price signals and flexibility enabled by a cap-and-trade program result in a least-cost solution to environmental problems and promote innovation.

Early program outcomes, such as the phasing out of leaded gasoline and the virtual elimination of acid rain, have led to widespread adoption of cap-and-trade throughout the world. The result has been creation of a new asset class—the environment—to join the traditional asset classes of stocks, bonds, real estate, foreign exchange, and tangible commodities.

Markets in emissions and use rights exist for a variety of pollutants and natural resources. They range from sulfur and carbon allowances, which were created to combat acid rain and global warming, to water and fishing rights, which fight drought and depletion of the ocean's resources. The commoditization of air and water has also been extended to catastrophe and weather risk. Finally, the commoditization of "sustainable stocks"—the equities of companies believed to be conducting environmentally sound or sustainable operations—into new indices has provided investors new ways to participate in these markets.

The purpose of this book is to introduce this new asset class to financial analysts, investors, and corporations. It is of interest to these readers because it allows them to profit or reduce costs while promoting environmental and social benefits. Here is a new way "to do well while doing good."

This book reflects economic theory and practical experience. The chapters will cover three broad asset classes: air and water, catastrophe and weather risk, and sustainability. It will demonstrate how these environmental asset classes are being incorporated into commodities and into fixed-income and equity instruments. The book concludes with some insights into the current state of this emerging asset class, some food for thought, and predictions about the class's future. We hope that after reading this book, the reader will walk away with a solid preliminary understanding of the promising and transformational investment category of environmental assets.

1. A Brief Survey of Environmental Asset Classes

Environmental asset classes are not a hope for tomorrow but a reality today. This new asset category promises to grow dramatically as the world focuses on sustainable development.[1] Examples of environmental assets are rights to emit local and regional pollutants, such as sulfur dioxide and nitrogen oxide; rights to emit global pollutants, such as carbon dioxide; renewable energy credits; water quality and quantity rights; and indices of sustainable corporate equities. This new asset class is the manifestation in securities markets of an emerging field of endeavor called "environmental finance." Environmental finance is the art and science of using economic incentives, financial tools, and market mechanisms to achieve desired environmental outcomes.[2]

The purpose of this chapter is to introduce financial analysts, investors, and corporate executives to this new asset class, which should interest readers for many reasons. From a corporate standpoint, businesses today have to be cognizant of, and prepare for, new kinds of corporate risks, including those arising from environmental problems and resource scarcity. These environmental risks include, among others, those related to production inputs (e.g., clean water for a beverage company), by-products of production (e.g., wastewater from chemical processing), and corporate social responsibility.

In addition, for companies to be competitive, their executives have to be aware of opportunities that environmental markets have to offer. Environmental asset classes allow businesses to pursue major new opportunities while simultaneously achieving their energy and environmental goals.

Similarly, to evaluate companies on the basis of their environmental performance, exposure to environmental risks, and response to environmental opportunities, financial analysts need to understand emerging environmental asset classes. Portfolio managers may also want to incorporate these new asset classes in their portfolios.

---

[1]The most commonly used definition of "sustainable development" appeared in the 1987 Brundtland Report: "development that meets the needs of the present without compromising the ability of future generations to meet their own needs." See UN, "Report of the World Commission on Environment and Development: Our Common Future," United Nations (1987). The Brundtland Commission (the World Commission on Environment and Development) was established by the United Nations in 1983.

[2]The term "environmental finance" was first adopted in an eponymous course offered by Richard L. Sandor at Columbia University in 1992. It helped ratify the academic underpinning of this growing new field. It has become widely used by other academic courses, industry publications, and conferences.

This chapter provides an overview of environment use rights, fixed-income securities, and equity instruments. It lays the framework for understanding the detailed discussion of the topics addressed in later chapters.

Emergence of the Environmental Asset Class

The first application of the innovative concept of cap-and-trade was the phasing out of lead-based gasoline in 1982. Although relatively small, this program was immensely successful and was important as a "proof of concept." The success of the lead phase-out program enabled the first large-scale environmental market in the United States—namely, the Environmental Protection Agency (EPA) Acid Rain Program. Implemented in the early 1990s, this program used the cap-and-trade market model to reduce sulfur and nitrogen oxide emissions from fossil-fuel combustion in electricity power plants. The environmental objectives of the Acid Rain Program were achieved with minimal costs relative to benefits. The implementation of the program was accompanied by the evolution of over-the-counter (OTC) spot and forward markets in emission allowances. A host of financial derivatives followed, including futures, options, and swaps.

Note that, in addition to providing a transparent price for the rights to pollute and flexibility in meeting environmental mandates for regulated entities, the Acid Rain Program promoted entrepreneurship, job creation, and market incentives for new technology. These intangibles clearly demonstrated the huge social benefits that can be accrued through well-designed environmental markets.

The acid rain markets led economists and policymakers to use cap-and-trade to combat a much larger problem: global warming. The passage of international and regional mandates to reduce greenhouse gases implicated in causing global warming served as an early catalyst for environmental financial markets. The global markets in trading carbon allowances are the largest and most successful application of the cap-and-trade model.

Parallel to the growth of emissions markets has been a push for more environmental disclosure from investors and public interest groups. Indeed, concerns about climate change liability have captured the attention of equity and debt analysts and corporate executives. This trend has produced growth in all aspects of environmental finance. In addition to emissions markets, we now have renewable energy certificates, energy-efficiency credits, and a developed market in sustainable stock indices. Corporations are also paying greater attention to satisfying their energy needs by using cleaner and more sustainable energy sources, leading to investment interest in that activity. Other emerging environmental markets—in water, biofuels, and ecosystems—are similarly promising.

The following section gives an overview of environmental asset classes discussed in detail later.

Environmental Asset Classes

Environmental asset classes include the securities or instruments created through the commoditization of environmental and natural resource assets, such as emissions rights and water; instruments arising from the monetization of specific environmental attributes, such as renewable energy or energy efficiency; and equity indices called "sustainable indices" to reflect the overall environmental performance of their constituent companies.

Sulfur Dioxide and Nitrogen Oxide Allowances. When coal is burned, four main pollutants are released into the atmosphere—oxides of sulfur, nitrogen, mercury, and carbon. The first two pollutants are associated with acid rain and smog. The prevalence of acid rain in the 1980s motivated the widespread application of cap-and-trade as a mechanism to solve that particular environmental problem. Emissions products in this category include sulfur dioxide (SO_2 or SO2) emissions futures and options contracts and nitrogen oxide (NOx or NOX) emissions futures and options contracts.[3]

The primary markets for trading these commodities are the IntercontinentalExchange and the Chicago Mercantile Exchange (CME). Variants of these kinds of contracts include products that are specific to a certain year's SO_2 or NOX emissions, referred to as vintages. These markets have long histories as the earliest emissions markets in existence. Market participants are utilities, industrial corporations, brokers, investment banks, and investment managers.

Carbon Dioxide Allowances. The widespread intellectual and political support of emissions trading was reflected in the Kyoto Protocol of 1997, which established several emissions-trading mechanisms. Industrialized countries that accepted the treaty agreed to legally binding commitments to reduce greenhouse gas (GHG) emissions. The European Union implemented the largest of the existing cap-and-trade markets for GHGs, with a volume of emissions in excess of 2.2 billion metric tons of carbon dioxide (CO_2) per year. In addition, two regional programs currently operate in the United States: the Regional Greenhouse Gas Initiative and the California cap-and-trade program, also known as AB 32 (i.e., Assembly Bill 32). China has set up seven pilot markets to reduce its carbon intensity, and India is about to begin its own markets to address energy efficiency.

GHG emissions products are a direct result of mandatory and voluntary programs to reduce GHG emissions. These markets are the largest category in environmental finance and are discussed in Chapter 4. At present, 10 regulated

---

[3]The first symbol shown is the chemical formula, and the second is the symbol usually used to refer to these substances in a financial context.

futures exchanges around the world offer derivative products in GHGs. Of these, the most popular marketplace is the IntercontinentalExchange (ICE), which accounts for more than 85% of regulated exchange-traded volumes. ICE currently offers futures and options products for the European Union Allowances (EUA), Certified Emission Reduction, and emission-reduction units. ICE EUA futures began in 2012 with an open interest of 560,520 and peaked at 1,226,797 (around 94% of ICE Brent futures) in December 2012 before declining.[4] Other prominent exchanges offering climate products are the CME, the Germany-based European Energy Exchange, and Norway-based Nord Pool. In addition to derivatives based on emissions products, a small set of financial products have emerged, including climate-based exchange-traded funds, carbon and clean energy indices, and structured financial instruments.

Renewable Energy and Energy-Efficiency Assets. This category of environmental finance, discussed in detail in Chapter 5, involves trading in environmental attributes. The renewable energy and energy-efficiency markets represent innovation in electricity wherein a specific "clean" attribute of power has been monetized.

The first set involves an interesting innovation in the power markets, renewable energy certificates (RECs). Also known as green certificates, green tags, or tradable renewable certificates, RECs represent the environmental attributes of the power produced from renewable energy projects and are sold separately from the electricity itself. RECs may be traded among regulated entities that have a mandate to include renewable power in a portion of their generation mix or may be traded by retail and corporate customers that wish to include renewable power in their consumption mix.

Already, national and regional REC markets are operating in many countries, including the United States, the United Kingdom, and Australia. Currently in the United States, about 29 states and the District of Columbia require utilities to include a certain percentage of renewable energy in their power generation mix. In addition, a voluntary market for RECs is growing, as is individual retail demand for green power.

The second set involves the development of energy-efficiency markets through energy-efficiency credits. Energy-efficiency credits are tradable instruments guaranteeing a certain amount of energy savings. These credits are most commonly generated in response to policy directives requiring improvements in energy-efficiency standards. Energy-efficiency credits are

---

[4]"Brent" is a reference to Brent crude oil, a major trading classification of sweet light crude oil. In 2012, ICE Brent became the world's largest crude oil futures contract in terms of volume.

increasingly being used as a policy tool to attain certain levels of energy efficiency in various economic sectors.

An example is India's Perform, Achieve and Trade program, which covers 478 plants in various sectors. Each plant has been assigned a specific reduction target in energy consumption compared with its baseline consumption (which is the average amount consumed between April 2007 and March 2010). The assigned target is to be attained by 2015. Plants that can achieve energy-efficiency gains beyond their reduction targets will receive energy saving certificates (ESCerts). Those that fail to meet their targets can buy ESCerts from other plants or pay a fine. This program is expected to have a significant impact on GHG emissions and energy efficiency.

Water Assets. The idea of treating water as an asset class is being driven by the fundamental need for water for human survival and the fact that the world is running out of usable clean water. Freshwater, which accounts for less than 1% of available water, is needed for food production, energy production, and most manufacturing processes. Chapter 6 discusses water as an environmental asset class. The chapter delves into both water quality and quantity issues and the associated financial risks and opportunities in this asset class. The various categories of water markets include the following:

- *Water quantity assets.* These markets involve trading in water permits that deliver a certain quantity of water at a certain time. Such permits are the most common in the existing water markets.

- *Water quality assets.* These markets involve trading in various nutrients and other water pollutants that are responsible for causing water quality problems. Most common are those in agricultural runoff, such as nitrogen and phosphorus, which can contaminate a local water resource. Water quality trading aims to reduce nutrient levels through trading of permits that limit the total amount of nutrients in the watershed.

- *Water temperature assets.* The development of creative regional markets regulating riparian water temperature in the western United States to protect local fishery resources serves as a reminder that many environmental outcomes can be achieved through properly designed markets.[5]

Catastrophic and Weather Event Assets. This category involves environmental markets designed to manage risks from weather conditions and such catastrophic events as hurricanes and earthquakes. The products

---

[5]"Riparian" refers to the interface between land and water, such as on the banks of a river.

include index-based futures and options contracts on weather outcomes and insurance products. The weather derivatives markets were valued at $11.8 billion in 2010 and were growing at a 20% annual rate.[6] Active weather contracts for several international cities are currently hosted by the CME. These markets are discussed in detail in Chapter 7.

Sustainability-Focused Portfolios. The traditional business model contains a tradeoff between a company's economic performance and its environmental performance. In other words, corporate profits are increased at the expense of the environment. A growing body of research suggests, however, that a company's environmental performance can enhance its long-term shareholder value and, therefore, be a good predictor of future economic performance.

This idea led to the emergence of sustainability-focused portfolios, mutual funds, and equity indices (detailed in Chapter 8). Ratings of corporate performance with respect to their carbon footprint, water use, and energy efficiency have emerged to enable portfolio managers to effectively screen for the environmental performances of companies. Such ratings are provided by CERES (developed by the California Resources Agency), the Carbon Disclosure Project (CDP), and the CDP Water Disclosure Project.

Sustainability approaches are also increasing inroads into the management of mutual funds. It is common for some funds to have sustainability-focused strategies. For example, the Neuberger Berman Socially Responsible Investment Fund screens for companies that demonstrate leadership in the environment, and the Firsthand Alternative Energy Fund invests primarily in equity securities of companies that are involved in developing alternative energy. Another strategy for sustainability-focused mutual funds is to avoid investing in companies that produce goods and services with negative social impacts, such as alcohol, tobacco, and weaponry companies. Finally, sustainability-related equity indices, such as the Dow Jones Sustainability Indices, have emerged to track the financial performance of selected companies identified as leaders in corporate sustainability. Such indices help financial analysts pick companies on the basis of their corporate sustainability performance and assess risks on the basis of the belief that long-term returns are correlated with the sustainability ratings of corporations.

Table 1.1 provides examples of environmental markets in existence today. The list indicates the vast array of financial innovations that have been spawned in a relatively new field.

---

[6]Unless otherwise noted, in this book the $ sign refers to the US dollar.

Table 1.1. Examples of Environmental Programs

Category/Name	Region	Commodity	Start Date	Value	Stage
Emissions					
SO$_2$ Trading Program	United States	SO$_2$	1990	$290M[a]	Mature (but with legal challenges)
Regional Clean Air Incentives Market (RECLAIM)	California	SO$_2$ and NOX	1994	$1.02B[b]	Mature
Regional Greenhouse Gas Initiative	Northeastern US states	CO$_2$	2003	$249M[c]	Mature
EU Emissions Trading Scheme (ETS)	European Union	GHG	Phase I: 2005–07, Phase II: 2008–12	$171.0B[d]	Mature
California Emissions Trading Program	California	CO$_2$	2013	$2.5B–$7.5B[e]	Nascent
South Korea Emissions Trading Scheme	South Korea	CO$_2$	2013–2015	NA	Proposal
China Emissions Trading Scheme	China	CO$_2$	2013	NA	Proposal
Emissions-related markets					
Reducing Emissions from Deforestation and Forest Degradation	Global	Offsets	2009	$85M[f]	Nascent
Certified Emission Reductions (Primary)	Global	Offsets	1997	$1B[g]	Mature
Verified Carbon Standard	Global	Offsets	2007	$1.7B	Developed
Energy efficiency/renewable fuels					
Perform, Achieve and Trade	India	Energy efficiency	2011	$144M[h]	Development
CRC (Carbon Reduction Commitment) Energy Efficiency Scheme	United Kingdom	Energy efficiency	2007	$68B[i]	Mature
Renewable identification numbers (RINs)	United States	Biofuel	2005	$8.7B[j]	Mature

(continued)

Table 1.1. Examples of Environmental Programs (continued)

Category/Name	Region	Commodity	Start Date	Value	Stage
Water					
Water quantity trading: Australia Water Trading	Australia	Water quantity allowances	1980–1990	$1.67B[k]	Mature
Water quality trading: Chesapeake Bay nutrient trading	Pennsylvania	Water quality credits	2010	$45M–$300M[l]	Nascent
Temperature credits (e.g., temperature TMDL [total maximum daily load])	Oregon	Water quality	2008	$3.2M[m]	In progress
Weather					
Weather derivatives	Global	Weather-related events (e.g., CME hurricane futures)	Late 1990s	$12B[n]	Mature
Catastrophe bonds	Global	Catastrophes	Mid-1990s	$15.6B[o]	Mature

NA = not available.

[a]The total value of the allowance market is a snapshot based on the average nominal price as of December 2010 ($19/ton) and the total allowance volume available for 2010 compliance. *Source:* EPA, "2010 Progress Report: Emission, Compliance, and Market Analyses," Environmental Protection Agency (October 2011): www.epa.gov/airmarkets/progress/ARPCAIR_downloads/ARPCAIR10_analyses.pdf.

[b]This number reflects the amount traded since RECLAIM was adopted. *Source:* Annual RECLAIM Audit Report for 2011 Compliance Year (1 March 2013).

[c]This number indicates the value, in US dollars, of transactions that occurred in 2011. *Source:* Molly Peters-Stanley and Katherine Hamilton, "Developing Dimension: State of the Voluntary Carbon Markets 2012," Ecosystem Marketplace and Bloomberg New Energy Finance (May 2012).

[d]This figure reflects the total transaction value in the EU ETS allowances in 2011. *Source:* "State and Trends of the Carbon Market 2012," Carbon Finance at the World Bank (May 2012).

[e]Estimates for the first year of the program (i.e., 2012). Market value is predicted to increase to $21.9 billion by 2020. *Source:* "Designing the Allocation Process for California's Greenhouse Gas Emissions Trading Program: The Multi-Billion Dollar Question," *Next 10* (December 2010).

[f]David Diaz, Katherine Hamilton, and Evan Johnson, "State of the Forest Carbon Markets 2011: From Canopy to Currency," Ecosystem Marketplace and Forest Trends (September 2011).

[g]"State and Trends of the Carbon Market 2011," Carbon Finance at the World Bank (June 2011).

Table 1.1. Examples of Environmental Programs (continued)

[h]Estimated market value by 2015.

[i]The next compliance period (2013–2017) requires the United Kingdom to limit its carbon emissions to 2,782 million metric tons of carbon dioxide equivalent. The price floor is currently set at £16/ton. Multiplying the two provides the indicative market size. For more program details, visit www.gov. uk. *Source:* Edward Craft, "United Kingdom: In Counsel—The New CRC Energy Efficiency Scheme Order 2013," Mondaq (May 2013): www.mondaq. com/x/238230/Energy+Law/In+Counsel+The+New+CRC+Energy+Efficiency+Scheme+Order+2013. Accessed 10 May 2013.

[j]According to a report by Goldman Sachs, approximately 15 billion RINs were issued in 2012. The RIN price today is around $0.58/RIN. Multiplying the two gives us the market size estimate. *Source:* "Americas: Energy: Oil—Refining," Goldman Sachs Group (25 March 2013).

[k]The figure reflects the total turnover of Australian water markets in 2011–2012. *Source:* "Australian Water Markets Report 2011–12," Australian Government National Water Commission (March 2013): http://nwc.gov.au/__data/assets/pdf_file/0008/29186/Introduction.pdf. Accessed 10 May 2013.

[l]This number is an estimate for how much the program can generate per year. *Source:* Cy Jones, Evan Branosky, Mindy Selman, and Michelle Perez, "How Nutrient Trading Could Help Restore the Chesapeake Bay," World Resources Institute (February 2010).

[m]This number reflects the total value of transactions in 2008. *Source:* Tracy Stanton, Marta Echavarria, Katherine Hamilton, and Caroline Ott, "The State of Watershed Payments: An Emerging Marketplace," Ecosystem Marketplace and Forest Trends (June 2010).

[n]*Source:* PricewaterhouseCoopers, "2011 Weather Risk Derivative Survey," Prepared for the Weather Risk Management Association (May 2011).

[o]This figure reflects the amount outstanding as of the end of 2012. *Source:* "Insurance-Linked Securities (ILS) Market Review 2012 and Outlook 2013," Munich Re (2013): www.munichre.com/app_pages/www/@res/pdf/reinsurance/business/non-life/financial_risks/ils-market-review-2012-and-outlook-2013-en.pdf. Accessed 10 May 2013.

Conclusion

Growth in environmental markets has helped integrate corporate climate and environmental risks and liabilities into the balance sheets of businesses. Climate risks and pollution are no longer under the exclusive purview of the environmental, health, and safety departments of companies but are also of interest to the finance and accounting departments. Environmental financial markets have helped corporations hedge and manage long-term business risks associated with environmental mandates. In addition, as the markets mature, the opportunity arises to use these financial tools as catalysts for achieving numerous environmental sustainability and social development goals. Just as corporations must adjust their business models in response to the climate challenge, those concerned with the health of the environment must inform and motivate societies around the world to adapt to an environmentally sound mode of living.

But why have these environmental markets flourished? They have flourished because of the existence of externalities and the efficacy of cap-and-trade in dealing with them. The next chapter will explain what externalities are and how cap-and-trade works.

2. Market Failures and Policy Responses

Economic theories and concepts are needed to understand the role of markets in addressing pollution. In this chapter, we analyze environmental problems from the perspective of market failure, explore several solutions to environmental problems, and provide numerical examples to illustrate the advantages of some of these solutions. Although most people would agree that market-based solutions are superior to command-and-control measures, debate continues regarding the desirability of market solutions versus taxes and subsidies.

Externalities, Property Rights, and Market Imperfections

Externalities are defined as spillover costs (negative) or benefits (positive) from the production of a good or service that accrue to individuals or entities not involved in the production process. Environmental pollution is widely cited in microeconomics as an example of a *negative externality*. Economists have long debated the proper societal responses for preventing and remedying this externality.

Externalities are most likely to occur where property rights are not clearly defined. Private and public entities that own resources outright are motivated to manage the resource properly because any gain or loss in the resource's value affects them directly. Resource owners will require that a polluter compensate them for any diminution in their resource's value; if the polluter does not compensate them, the resource owners will not allow the resource to be used. By this process, resources are conserved in a pure property system. (Of course, it is not possible or desirable for some resources, such as air, to be owned outright; we will get to that issue later.) Note that property rights need not be private in order to achieve desirable outcomes. As long as the property rights are enforced and private reasons, either legal or economic, exist to maintain the resource, a socially desirable outcome can be achieved. Thus, well-defined property rights are central to our preferred approach to managing externalities.

When polluters do not have to compensate society for the pollution caused by their production processes, they do not have an incentive to reduce pollution and will produce at levels that maximize their individual profits. In the absence of fair pricing of externalities (fair compensation for the resource owners), the level of production is usually above the socially optimal level. By polluting, producers impose costs on society in the form of health hazards and environmental degradation.

Some examples may be helpful. Consider air and water pollution caused by a factory. The private profit–maximizing actions of the factory may result in negative effects on individuals in the vicinity of the plant. Local water and air quality may deteriorate from pollutants released into local lakes, rivers, and the atmosphere. In contrast, a beekeeper who is located next to a farm can produce positive externalities. The bees help pollinate and, therefore, increase the crop productivity of the farm.

All externalities are a form of market failure. Market failures occur when the pricing mechanism does not take into account all of the actual costs and benefits of producing or consuming a good. For example, suppose a widget factory is located next to a town and a lake. It makes a product from the power it generates by burning fossil fuels, and the burning of the fossil fuels releases sulfur dioxide into the atmosphere locally, which causes respiratory problems in the local population. Furthermore, suppose the factory uses freshwater in its manufacturing process and this water is returned to the lake filled with toxic chemicals. **Table 2.1** presents the output of widgets, the price of widgets, the total revenue, the total cost of producing the widgets, and the social cost of damage from the pollution of air and water.

In this example, the profit-maximizing production for the firm is 50 widgets, which gives the firm a profit of $90. For the surrounding town, the value of these widgets is −$10 (i.e., Profit − Cost of pollution [or $90 − $100]). Thus, 50 widgets is not the socially optimal level of production. If the firm had to pay for its pollution, the optimum output for the firm would be 40 widgets because this amount yields the highest profit after paying for pollution. In this example, the market imperfection of not pricing the emissions results in an undesirable social outcome.

Table 2.1. How Private Optima Diverge from Social Optima

Widget Output (units)	Widget Price	Total Revenues (units × price)	Total Cost of Production	Profit (revenues − cost)	Emissions (tons)	Cost of Pollution	Profit after Paying for Pollution
10	$10	$100	$60	$40	$20	$30	$10
20	10	200	150	50	40	40	10
30	10	300	240	60	60	45	15
40[a]	10	400	320	80	80	60	20
50[b]	10	500	410	90	100	100	−10
60	10	600	660	−60	120	180	−240

[a]Social optimum.
[b]Private optimum.

Solutions to Externalities

This simple example provides insight into the policy tools available to reach the optimal societal production of 40 widgets. Three policy tools that can be used to achieve this target are (1) command-and-control, (2) subsidies and/or taxes, and (3) cap-and-trade.

Command-and-control in its most basic form would involve a law that limits the firm's production to no more than 40 widgets. In a more complex form, the local environmental regulator could require the firm to install technology that reduces its emissions. The choice of these alternatives would depend on the transaction costs. In this case, the regulator would weigh the cost of enforcing and administering these command-and-control measures against the benefit to the firm and society.

Another alternative is to impose a tax on the output of widgets or on the amount of pollution emitted. In this particular example, a tax of $1.08 per widget would result in a profit-maximizing production of 40 widgets. **Table 2.2** extends the example in Table 2.1 by showing the possible outcome of imposing a tax on production units.

If each widget produced resulted in 2 tons of pollutants, then a tax of $0.60 per ton would achieve the same result.

Table 2.3 demonstrates the outcomes of levying a tax on the externality itself.

Table 2.2. Taxing the Production

Widget Output (units)	Price per Widget	Total Revenues (units × price)	Tax ($1.08/widget)	Total Cost of Production	Profit (revenues – tax – cost)
10	$10	$100	$11	$60	$29
20	10	200	22	150	28
30	10	300	32	240	28
40	10	400	43	320	37
50	10	500	54	410	36
60	10	600	65	660	−125

Table 2.3. Taxing the Externality

Widget Output (units)	Widget Price	Total Revenues (units × price)	Total Cost of Production	Profit (revenues – cost)	Emissions (tons)	Pollution Tax ($0.6/ton)	Profit after Paying for Pollution
10	$10	$100	$60	$40	20	$12	$28
20	10	200	150	50	40	24	26
30	10	300	240	60	60	36	24
40	10	400	320	80	80	48	32
50	10	500	410	90	100	60	30
60	10	600	660	−60	120	72	−132

Another alternative is cap-and-trade. Consensus has grown among the scientific and environmental communities that such market mechanisms as cap-and-trade are viable tools to manage environmental challenges.

A cap-and-trade program establishes limits on overall emissions at the company level. Companies with low abatement costs (costs incurred with elimination of pollutants) can reduce emissions below their required limits and sell the excess reductions. Companies with high abatement costs may buy those excess reductions to comply with their own regulatory limits. The market allows for efficient use of the limited resource (environmental goods) and yields a price that signals the value society places on use of the environment. The following example can also be applied to the widget factory if one assumes that the widget factory and the town are two separate entities with different marginal costs of pollution abatement.

The concept of emissions trading stems from Ronald Coase's theory of social cost.[7] It has been well articulated by John H. Dales.[8] The argument is that by assigning clear property rights, the market can play a valuable role in ensuring that these rights go toward their most efficient use. The initial allocation of allowances, if there are no transaction costs, is irrelevant from the point of view of economic efficiency.[9] The initial allocation of allowances may have implications, however, related to income distribution.

These alternatives are being debated in the United States and internationally. Such market-based solutions as cap-and-trade are less costly than command-and-control measures, which usually do not cause the property rights to flow into their highest valued use. Appendix A provides a numerical illustration that demonstrates the superiority of cap-and-trade to command-and-control. Although cap-and-trade and taxes can achieve the same results, given very narrow assumptions, we regard cap-and-trade as the preferred alternative.

We want to emphasize that the purpose of this book is to inform financial professionals about the role of markets in addressing pollution and, concomitantly, educate readers about the opportunities the markets provide. Environmental and emissions markets represent new opportunities for both sellers and buyers. To illustrate the growing importance of market-based mechanisms, the next section will look at some of the historical uses of these mechanisms to achieve environmental objectives.

---

[7] Ronald H. Coase, "The Problem of Social Cost," *Journal of Law and Economics*, vol. 3 (1960):1–44.
[8] John H. Dales, *Pollution, Property & Prices* (Toronto: University of Toronto Press, 1968).
[9] This principle is known as the "Coase theorem."

Early Applications of Market-Based Mechanisms to Environmental Problems

For most of the 1960s and early 1970s, command-and-control was the preferred measure among federal regulators to deal with pollution, as shown by the Clean Air Act of 1970. Regulators not only set environmental goals; they also imposed industry-wide standards that applied to all companies regardless of the cost of compliance. Since the introduction of federal pollution-control regulations, however, economists have advocated the allocation of property rights to environmental wastes as a cheaper alternative to traditional command-and-control measures.

The Environmental Protection Agency (EPA) began experimenting with emissions trading in 1974 when it adopted "netting"—a policy that allows a company to net the increased emissions from one source against reductions in another source at the same facility. Before netting was introduced, companies had to register all new plants as a "new source" under the Clean Air Act, which could be costly. After netting was introduced, multiple sources were treated as one large source. Netting resulted in an aggregated cost savings between $525 million and $12 billion from 1974 to 1984, according to Hahn and Hester.[10]

Similarly, the EPA introduced "offsets" in 1976 when it became clear that many of the nation's Air Quality Control Regions (federally designated areas that must meet and maintain federal ambient air quality standards) could not attain the national ambient air quality standards by the deadline. The introduction of offsets allowed the construction of new stationary sources of emissions in areas that could not meet the standards as long as the new emissions were offset by reductions at existing sources. By 1988, 2,000 offset transactions had already taken place. The savings are difficult to quantify, but the fact that these transactions occurred at all illustrates the intrinsic economic need that offsets fulfill.

In 1979, the EPA encouraged companies to use "bubbles" to cut the cost of regulations. Although a single plant may contain many sources of pollution, a bubble policy may include facilities owned by various firms and treats their emissions as if they were from a single source. Thus, a bubble policy essentially allows the implicit transfer of emission from smokestack to smokestack within the bubble. This policy tool has resulted in $435 million in savings.[11] Also in 1979, the EPA introduced "banking"—a policy measure whereby companies can save or "bank" their emission credits for future use.

---

[10]Robert Hahn and Gordon Hester, "Where Did All the Markets Go? An Analysis of EPA's Emissions Trading Program," *Yale Journal on Regulation*, vol. 6, no. 1 (Winter 1989):109–153.
[11]Hahn and Hester, "Where Did All the Markets Go?" op cit.

Although none of these measures introduced by the EPA constitutes a trading program, together, they paved the way for the first application of cap-and-trade in 1982: the phasing out of lead-based gasoline. The EPA launched a trading scheme for lead use across refineries in 1982. The "cap" was set at 1.1 grams of lead per gallon. This trading scheme included the banking feature, so refineries that reduced lead more than they needed to could store the lead rights for later use. EPA analysis shows that the program resulted in an estimated savings of about $250 million per year.

These early programs paved the way for SO_2 and NOX trading, as demonstrated in the next chapter.

3. Acid Rain Pollutants as an Asset Class

"Acid rain" is a broad term referring to a mixture of wet and dry deposition from the atmosphere containing higher-than-normal amounts of nitric and sulfuric acids. It has been virtually eradicated in the United States. Emissions of sulfur dioxide (SO_2 or SO2) and nitrogen oxides (NOx or NOX), the main precursors of acid rain, have declined more than 75% from their 1980 levels.[12] In addition, the reductions in SO2 and NOX have dramatically reduced health costs associated with lung disease—the main impact of SO2 and NOX emissions on humans—at a minimal cost to the economy. The eradication of acid rain helped reduce smog, prevented damage to forests, and reduced acidification of lakes and rivers.

How did this happen? A cap-and-trade model, the Acid Rain Program, enabled by the Clean Air Act Amendments of 1990 put a price on SO2 emissions for the first time. In doing so, it lowered the transaction costs associated with reducing emissions that cause acid rain. The success of the program demonstrated that the cap-and-trade mechanism is not only theoretically sound but also practical. It provided empirical evidence that was useful in extending cap-and-trade to other pollutants, such as NOX—a significant contributor to both acid rain and ground-level ozone (smog)—and carbon dioxide (CO_2), the principal cause of global warming.

Pricing pollution provided benefits to both the private and public sectors. The price signal of SO2 allowances gave utilities and industrial corporations a way of achieving the mandated reductions in the most cost-effective way. Financial analysts, with the aid of these price signals, were able to evaluate investment opportunities in the technologies used for reducing SO2 emissions and in related companies, such as investor-owned utilities, coal companies that could benefit from increased use of low-sulfur coal, and manufacturers of pollution-control technologies. Financial institutions also saw an opportunity to benefit from the marketing, financing, and brokering of SO2 allowances.

This chapter provides an overview of the Acid Rain Program. Of the two acid rain pollutants, this chapter will focus on the main pollutant, SO2. The main drivers of the SO2 allowance market and lessons learned from dealing with it are also applicable to the NOX market.[13]

---

[12]US EPA, "Clean Air Interstate Rule, Acid Rain Program and Former NOx Budget Trading Program 2011 Progress Report," US Environmental Protection Agency (November 2012): www.epa.gov/airmarkets/progress/ARPCAIR11_01.html.

[13]For a complete description of the NOX program, visit www.epa.gov/airmarkets/progsregs/nox/index.html.

Causes of Acid Rain and Public Policy Responses

Combustion of coal for power generation leads to the release of sulfur dioxide and nitrogen oxides into the atmosphere. Because these gases are the principal precursors of acid rain and its damage to lakes and forests, as well as fine particulates that pose human health risks, emissions from coal power generation constitutes a negative externality. As indicated in Chapter 2, this negative externality was not priced or significantly constrained by law during most of the 20th century; indeed, electrical power was generated with little or no regard for its externalities. Thus, a large volume of pollutants resulted.

Increased electricity demand from the mid-20th century on caused utilities to build new coal-fired power plants (then, the cheapest source of electricity) and burn more coal in general to meet the new demand. In some regions, such as in the midwestern United States, utilities burned unusually large amounts of coal because power plants were located near coal deposits. As a result, atmospheric emissions of SO_2 and NO_X increased substantially.

The level of SO_2 emissions also became geographically more widespread because of local laws. These laws, in an attempt to alleviate local air quality problems in the 1970s, required utilities to construct tall smokestacks. Utilities in the United States constructed more than 429 smokestacks—many of them higher than 500 feet—on coal-fired boilers, causing winds to carry the emissions to other states.[14] As a consequence, the vast majority of urban areas in the 1980s attained the local ambient air quality standards for SO_2. The smokestack remedy for local problems, however, contributed to the deterioration of air quality at a regional level. Released high in the atmosphere, SO_2 emissions from coal plants traveled hundreds of miles and increased acid rain.[15] This circumstance caused large increases in acidification, particularly in the eastern half of the United States.

Public concern over these environmental issues motivated legislators to pass the Clean Air Act Amendments (CAAA) of 1990. The US program for trading SO_2 emission allowances was enabled by Title IV of the CAAA. The Acid Rain Program required electric utilities to reduce their SO_2 emissions by about 50% from 1980 levels. For the total electricity sector, SO_2 emissions were approximately 17.5 million tons in 1980, and the reduction target was approximately 3.5 million tons over a five-year period with a further 5 million tons mandated in the second phase of the program. The law directed the US Environmental Protection Agency to implement a phased-in program.

---

[14]James L. Regens and Robert W. Rycroft, *The Acid Rain Controversy* (Pittsburgh: University of Pittsburgh Press, 1988).

[15]Dallas Burtraw and Sarah Jo Fueyo Szambelan, "U.S. Emissions Trading Markets for SO_2 and NO_X," Resources for the Future Discussion Paper No. 09-40 (October 2009): http://papers.ssrn.com/sol3/papers.cfm?abstract_id=1490037. Accessed 2 May 2013.

Results of the Public Policy Responses

Title IV successfully reduced emissions of SO_2 and NOX from power generation (i.e., the sources covered by the Acid Rain Program). It was complemented by subsequent cap-and-trade programs, specifically the NOx Budget Trading Program and the Clean Air Interstate Rule (CAIR). The result of these efforts was a reduction in SO2 emissions to 5.2 million tons in 2010, an amount 67% lower than 1990 emissions and below the original 2010 statutory cap of 8.95 million tons. Another result was a reduction in NOX emissions to 2.1 million tons in 2010, an amount 67% lower than 1990 emissions and substantially better than the Title IV goal.[16] **Figure 3.1** illustrates the reductions made relative to the targeted cap.

The emission reductions achieved under the Acid Rain Program and its offshoots have contributed to measurable improvements in air quality, decreases in acid deposition, the beginning of recovery in some acid-sensitive lakes and streams, and improvements in visibility (air clarity). A report of the National Acid Precipitation Assessment Program to Congress estimated that the human health benefits of improved air quality were in the range of

---

[16]US EPA, "Clean Air Interstate Rule," op cit. Accessed 1 May 2013.

Figure 3.1.   Acid Rain Program Results

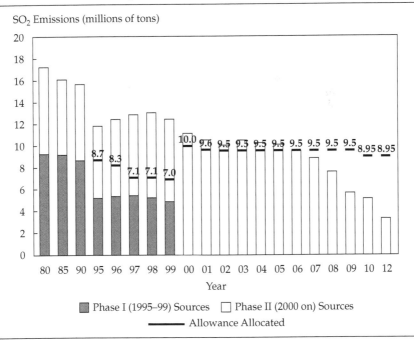

Source: US EPA, "Clean Air Interstate Rule," op cit.

$170 billion to $430 billion in 2010 alone.[17] The EPA estimated in 2010 that 20,000–50,000 lives are saved annually by reductions in the number of diseases associated with acid rain.[18] Because the cost of the program was estimated at about $3 billion, its net benefit has been in the range of $167 billion to $427 billion, and thus, it has made a significant contribution to GDP and job creation. Moreover, this benefit number does not capture the number of lives that were saved by the program or other, more intangible benefits, such as improved visibility and ecological conditions.

Enabling and Implementing the Acid Rain Program

The sulfur dioxide reduction legislation in the CAAA simultaneously performed three functions: (1) It standardized an environmental commodity by creating a legally authorized property right (an allowance to emit 1 ton of sulfur dioxide), (2) it produced the "evidence of ownership," and (3) it established the infrastructure for the efficient transfer of titles of ownership. These enabling functions created the infrastructure for a market.

The vast majority of entities covered by the Acid Rain Program were power plants (mostly, investor-owned utilities). To a lesser degree, entities included large industrial producers that were major users of coal, such as BP Amoco and International Paper.

The law directed the EPA to implement a phased-in program that first targeted 110 large emitting plants (which comprised more than 400 fuel-consuming power plant *units*) for the years 1995–1999. Starting in 2000, Phase II extended the limits to all fossil-fueled power plants larger than 25 megawatt capacity. Eventually, more than 3,200 units were regulated.

Power plants were allocated a 30-year stream of tradable allowances, each worth 1 ton of SO2. In passing the CAAA, Congress codified into law much of the economic theory of environmental finance described in the previous chapter. In just 15 short pages, Congress specified the emissions baseline, reduction targets, and entities covered by the program. The salient features are as follows:[19]

- *Phases and reductions.* Title IV of the CAAA set a goal of reducing annual SO2 emissions to a level 10 million tons below 1980 levels from all sources

---

[17]Douglas A. Burns, Jason A. Lynch, Bernard J. Cosby, Mark E. Fenn, and Jill S. Baron, "National Acid Precipitation Assessment Program Report to Congress 2011: An Integrated Assessment," US EPA Clean Air Markets Division (January 2012).

[18]US EPA, "Highlights from the Clean Air Act 40th Anniversary Celebration," US Environmental Protection Agency: www.epa.gov/air/caa/40th_highlights.html. Accessed 1 May 2013.

[19]US EPA, "Acid Rain Program," US EPA Clean Air Markets Division (25 July 2012): www.epa.gov/airmarkets/progsregs/arp/basic.html.

(8.4 million tons below 1980 levels from power plants). To achieve these reductions, the law required a two-phase reduction program. Phase I began in 1995, and Phase II began in 2000.

- *Allowance allocation.* Phase I required 100 power plants to reduce their emissions to a level equivalent to the product of an emissions rate of 2.5 pounds of SO_2/mmBTU × an average of their 1985–87 fuel use.[20] Phase II required approximately 2,000 utilities to reduce their emissions to a level equivalent to the product of an emissions rate of 1.2 pounds of SO_2/mmBTU × the average of their 1985–87 fuel use. Each allowance permitted a power plant to emit 1 ton of SO_2 per year.

- *Allowance registry.* Regulated entities held their allowances in the EPA-administered electronic allowance-tracking registry. The allowance registry facilitated transfer of the allowances from one account to another. Allowances were serialized and designated by vintage year, which denoted the first year they could be used for compliance.

- *Annual reconciliation (compliance).* For each ton of SO2 emitted in a given year, one allowance was retired; that is, it could no longer be used. Allowances could be bought, sold, or banked for use in subsequent years. At the end of each year, sources were granted a 60-day grace period to ensure that they had sufficient allowances to match their SO_2 emissions during the previous year. If they needed to, they could buy allowances during the grace period. Sources could sell allowances that exceeded their emissions or bank them for use in future years.

- *Allowance trading.* SO_2 allowance trading minimized compliance costs, and because unused allowances could be sold to other program participants, the system encouraged emitters to reduce emissions *beyond* required levels.

- *Flexible compliance.* Each source could choose the most efficient way to reduce its SO_2 emissions. Options were installing new control technology, switching to lower-sulfur fuel, or optimizing existing controls.

- *Stringent monitoring.* Each source had to continuously measure and record its emissions of SO_2, NOX, and CO_2, as well as heat input, volumetric flow, and opacity. Most emissions were measured by a continuous emissions-monitoring system.

- *Automatic penalties and enforcement.* Any source that failed to hold enough allowances to match its SO_2 emissions for the previous year had to pay the EPA an automatic penalty of \$2,000 per ton of emissions in excess

---

[20]mmBTU = millions of British thermal units.

of allowances held. The source also had to immediately surrender to the EPA an amount of allowances, issued for the year the payment was due, equaling the tons of excess emissions.

The program required the EPA to conduct an annual allowance auction of current vintage (spot) and seven-year forward allowances. This auction was intended to facilitate market transactions of allowances and achieve price discovery. The mechanism involved auctioning 2.8% of the allowances allocated to the utilities in a competitive market and returned the proceeds to the individual utilities.

The clear and transparent guidelines set by the Acid Rain Program enabled the development of an active market for SO_2 allowances. In fact, over-the-counter trades in forwards and options occurred before the EPA registry was operational and the program went into effect. Organized exchanges entered when the Chicago Board of Trade (CBOT), on behalf of the EPA, competitively won the right to conduct the annual auctions of the spot and forward allowances. **Figure 3.2** details the clearing price of the spot and forward allowances at these annual auctions.

Price History of Acid Rain Program and Its Determinants

Liquid markets and transparent prices contributed to allowing power plants to choose the best option to comply with the Acid Rain Program regulations. In other words, plant operators could compare the risks and costs of

Figure 3.2.   Spot and Forward SO$_2$ Auction Results (1993–2012)

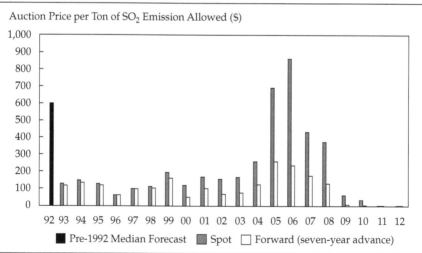

Auction Price per Ton of SO$_2$ Emission Allowed ($)

■ Pre-1992 Median Forecast   ▨ Spot   ☐ Forward (seven-year advance)

Source: US EPA, "Annual Auction," US EPA Clean Air Markets Division (26 March 2013): www.epa.gov/airmarkets/trading/auction.html.

the technological solutions with the allowance price. The pricing of SO2 pollution also led to enormous opportunities for financial institutions and market makers to earn a profit. Given the importance of price in this program, we provide an overview of the program's price history and how price was determined.

Initial Price Forecasts. Experts estimated that these emissions rights would command a high premium. (Some initial estimates ran as high as $1,500 per ton.)[21] Pre-1992 estimates of forecasted prices for sulfur emission allowances ranged from $309 (Resource Data International) to $981 (United Mine Workers of America).[22] **Table 3.1** provides a summary of these early estimates.

Because of the uncertainty of a new program, the initial price forecasts were vastly different for various studies, as indicated by Table 3.1. Although the average cost of achieving SO2 reductions through a scrubber installation was approximately $600 per ton, analysts' forecasts of this price spanned an unexpectedly wide range. A scrubber is a chemical factory built near the smokestack. The flue gas is passed through a limestone mix that removes the sulfur. Uncertainty about scrubber costs for retrofits was another reason the cost estimates were so high, and few believed that low-sulfur coal would become prevalent and relatively cheap.[23]

If the price of the allowances is less than the cost of the scrubber technology, then compliance should be reached using purchasing allowances.

---

[21]On 10 March 1997, EPA Administrator Carol Browner argued, "During the 1990 debate on the Acid Rain Program, industry initially projected the cost of an emission allowance to be $1500 per ton of sulfur dioxide. . . . Today, those allowances are selling for less than $100"; see "New Initiatives in Environmental Protection," *Commonwealth* (31 March 1997).

[22]Robert W. Hahn and Carol A. May, "The Behavior of the Allowance Market: Theory and Evidence." *Electricity Journal*, vol. 7 (March 1994):2, 28–37.

[23]The source of this information is the authors' conversation with Bruce Braine, vice president of strategic policy analysis at American Electric Power.

Table 3.1. Pre-1992 Forecasts of Phase I SO$_2$ Allowance Prices

Source	Price Forecast ($/ton)
United Mine Workers of America	$981
Ohio Coal Development Office	785
Electric Power Research Institute	688
Sierra Club	446
American Electric Power	392
Resource Data International	309

Source: Hahn and May, "Behavior of the Allowance Market," op cit.

Conversely, if the price of the allowances is higher than the cost of the technology, then a user should install the scrubber. Therefore, it would have been reasonable to purchase allowances at prices significantly below the $600 forecast. Early OTC trades occurred between $180 and $300.[24] Those prices suggest that purchasing allowances was the correct investment decision. It was correct in the long term but wrong in the short term. The first auction in 1993 had a spot market clearing price of $131. Prices continued to fall, reaching a low of $65 in 1996. Thereafter, prices rose until 2003.

By the end of 2004, prices had risen to $700, primarily because of the impending promulgation of the CAIR, which would significantly lower the SO2 cap by requiring surrender of additional allowances for each ton of emissions. This price rise was exacerbated by an increase in demand for coal-fired generation in response to an increase in natural gas prices and electricity demand. The buyers of this asset class at the outset of the program would have been handsomely rewarded.

Price Determinants in the Long Term. Over the long term, the drivers of price in this asset class have been railroad deregulation and the emergence of Powder River Basin coal, scrubber technology and fuel mix, improvements in the mining of low-sulfur eastern US coal, the banking provisions in the Acid Rain Program, and the impact of regulatory changes and legislative uncertainty.

▓ *Railroad deregulation and Powder River Basin coal.* The deregulation of the railroad industry was a contributing factor to the persistence of low allowance prices. The resultant competition among the major railroads for long-haul traffic from the Powder River Basin (PRB) in Wyoming and Montana to the midwestern United States was particularly fierce. The ability to ship low-sulfur coal from the PRB to places east of the Mississippi River at low rates prompted utilities to modify their boilers and switch from high-sulfur and medium-sulfur coals to coals containing much lower sulfur from the western United States. The choice was not always binary: Blending of eastern bituminous and western subbituminous types of coal was also prevalent. The burning of subbituminous coal emits less SO_2 and NOX than the burning of bituminous coal.

The effort to find cheaper emission-reduction options also led to experimentation that improved understanding and increased the use of fuel blending

---

[24]The first publicized trade was of 10,000 allowances at $265 per allowance from Wisconsin Power and Light Company to the Tennessee Valley Authority; see Frank Edward Allen, "Tennessee Valley Authority Is Buying Pollution Rights from Wisconsin Power," *Wall Street Journal* (11 May 1992):A12. The second was a trade of 25,000 allowances from Alcoa to Ohio Edison for $300 per allowance; see Joan E. Rigdon, "Alcoa Unit Arranges $7.5 Million Sale of Pollution Allowances to Ohio Edison," *Wall Street Journal* (1 July 1992):A6.

and the ability to use large amounts of PRB coal without incurring substantial capital costs and/or reducing combustion rates at power plants. This ability, in turn, reduced the cost of reducing emissions.

■ *Scrubber technology and fuel mix.* The cost and efficiency of new emissions-control equipment played an important role in keeping emissions allowance prices at low levels. Because SO_2 scrubbers typically reduce emissions by 90% or more, each installed scrubber can free up significant quantities of SO2 allowances.[25]

Scrubbing technology has improved and installation costs have fallen over time, making scrubbing the economical choice for more plants. The cost of installing and operating scrubbers varies from plant to plant, with upfront costs reaching into the hundreds of millions of dollars. Installation time can range from one to three years.[26]

Note that the regulatory treatment of costs of installing scrubbers influences the extent to which this compliance option is elected. State utility regulatory treatment that allows full cost recovery and an adequate return on investment of the costs of building and operating scrubbers encourages scrubber adoption. Thus, such treatments reduce allowance consumption and possibly increase available supply.

■ *Productivity improvements in low-sulfur eastern coal mining.* During the 1990s, substantial improvements in coal mining productivity occurred in mines in both the eastern and western United States.[27] This change allowed substantial increases in the production—and reductions in the prices—of low-sulfur coal. Coupled with the increased technological ability to mix high- and low-sulfur fuels, the improvements also meant that utilities had access to cheaper fuel sources closer to home. The allowance markets had a positive impact in forcing low-sulfur coal producers in the eastern states to compete with their western counterparts.

■ *Banking.* The Acid Rain Program provided emission sources with temporal flexibility through banking. It created an incentive for polluters to decrease emissions below allowable levels sooner than required, resulting in human health and environmental benefits occurring earlier than expected. Banking delivered liquidity, provided a cushion for price volatility, and created a safety mechanism for unforeseen market events. For example, over the five years of Phase I, regulated sources reduced emissions 10.5 million metric

---

[25]Chicago Climate Exchange, *The Sulfur Dioxide Emission Allowance Trading Program: Market Architecture, Market Dynamics and Pricing* (Chicago: Chicago Climate Exchange, 2004), p. 16.
[26]Chicago Climate Exchange, *Sulfur Dioxide Emission Allowance Trading Program*, op cit.
[27]US EIA, "Annual Energy Review 2011," US Energy Information Administration (September 2012): www.eia.gov/totalenergy/data/annual/pdf/aer.pdf.

tons more than required and were able use those banked allowances to cushion the effect of the declining cap in Phase II.[28]

▨ *Regulatory changes and legislative uncertainty.* Regulatory changes (such as tightened SO_2 emissions limits) and legislative uncertainty (such as inaction by the legislative body, which forced action by executive mandate that was eventually challenged in courts) can and did have an impact on the SO_2 emission allowance market—in both the long and the short term.[29]

As demonstrated throughout this book, emissions markets are extremely dependent on policy developments. Even though enabling legislation in the CAAA gave birth to the Acid Rain Program, regulatory uncertainty and court battles have, since 2008, greatly damaged the functioning of a cap-and-trade system in the Acid Rain Program.

As the Acid Rain Program entered its first decade, various proposals to tighten the cap were made. For example, in 1997, Senator Daniel P. Moynihan (D-NY) proposed legislation that would have reduced the SO_2 cap by 50%. Then, in 2002, the George W. Bush Administration proposed the Clear Skies Act, which would have tightened the SO_2 cap by 65%. Finally, in 2005, in the absence of congressional action, the Bush Administration promulgated the CAIR, which proposed a stringent cap on SO_2 emissions of 70% below their 2003 level. These actions caused a run-up in prices.

In 2006, however, North Carolina, a few other states, and a few utilities sued the EPA, arguing that the interstate trading allowed under CAIR was inconsistent with a provision of the Clean Air Act of 2003. In July 2008, the Circuit Court of Appeals for the District of Columbia ruled on this lawsuit by vacating CAIR completely. This ruling basically invalidated the core principle of the cap-and-trade system that had been enabled by the CAAA. In one day, SO2 prices plummeted from $315 to $115. Neither the outgoing Bush Administration nor the incoming Barack Obama Administration challenged the ruling, and Congress was unable to provide a simple legislative fix. Given the unlikely scenario that more stringent caps would be put into place, along with mounting regulatory uncertainty, SO_2 prices collapsed. This uncertainty depressed allowance prices to $65 by March 2009. In the EPA auction, future vintage allowances sold for $6.65.

In 2010, the Obama Administration proposed a replacement of CAIR. The objective was to limit annual SO_2 and NOX emissions in 28 states. The proposed rule established state-specific emissions caps for power plant

---

[28]Jeremy Schreifels and Sam Napolitano, "Efficient, Effective, and Credible Cap and Trade: Lessons Learned from the U.S. Acid Rain Program" (2007): www.caep.org.cn/english/paper/Lesson-from-US-Emission-Trading-Program-Edited-by-Jeremy.pdf. Accessed 1 May 2013.
[29]Another type of regulatory impact arises from regulatory changes related to other pollutants. Because burning coal releases carbon dioxide, sulfur dioxide, nitrogen oxides, and mercury, regulation of any of these pollutants may have an impact on the others.

emissions but limited interstate trading. The rule was finalized as the Cross-State Air Pollution Rule (CSAPR, or "Caspar," as it is commonly called), which allowed for intrastate trading but only limited trading between two groups of states. This rule was also challenged in court, and in August 2012, the DC Circuit Court vacated CSAPR and ordered the EPA to keep CAIR in force pending a review of CSAPR. In March 2013, the Obama Administration appealed the decision to the Supreme Court.

The courts struck down CSAPR and are forcing the EPA to develop a replacement rule, which will take several years at least. In the interim, CAIR will remain in place.

What is driving further SO_2 reductions, in actuality, is the Mercury and Air Toxics Standards rule that sets limits for new power plants.[30] As a result, CAIR is no longer binding.[31]

The importance of the impact of sovereign risk on the prices of environmental assets cannot be overstated. This recurring theme will be further discussed in Chapter 4.

Price Determinants in the Short Term. Factors that affect electricity demand and the composition of electricity supply affect allowance consumption and have the potential to significantly influence SO_2 allowance prices. Utilities may burn more coal in a short period for three main reasons: weather, demand for power from the various sectors, and the price of competing fuels.

▓ *Seasonal weather patterns and natural disasters.* Short-term fluctuations in total electricity production arise from variations in weather conditions (hot summer days, cold winter days) and economic activity, particularly industrial production. SO_2 emissions tend to be highest during the summer quarter, reflecting the system-wide peak load associated with the operation of air conditioners. The second-highest quarter for SO_2 emissions is the winter quarter. These patterns make clear that SO_2 allowance consumption is driven by the degree of weather extremity during summer and winter. Market analysts may consider heating-degree days and cooling-degree days in major coal-based regions to be a factor in assessing SO_2 allowance prices. Another factor is lack of rainfall, which can decrease power output from hydroelectric dams.

Natural disasters, such as hurricanes, may damage facilities that produce gas, thereby driving gas prices higher. Utilities then change from gas to coal, thereby increasing emissions and the demand for allowances.

---

[30]US EPA, "Fact Sheet: Updates of the Limits for New Power Plants under the Mercury and Air Toxics Standards (MATS)," US Environmental Protection Agency (28 March 2013): www.epa.gov/mats/pdfs/20130328fs.pdf.
[31]Conversation with Bruce Braine.

■ *Competing energy sources and fuel switching.* In the case of SO_2, nearly all allowance consumption is related to coal-based electricity production. With generation from natural gas–fired plants increasing, natural gas has become an easy alternative for utilities with fuel-switching ability. The decline in natural gas prices since 2011 has motivated power generators to switch to gas-fired plants instead of other electricity-generation resources. The flexibility to switch between coal- and gas-fired power generation is generally a factor reflected in SO2 emission allowance prices.

Figure 3.3 highlights the impact of some of the short-term and long-term price drivers on the price of allowances. Early low prices for allowances were a result of switching from high- to low-sulfur coal and installation of scrubbers. The subsequent price increase is the result of the increase in industrial activity and the Clear Skies announcement. Also, exogenous effects, such as Hurricanes Katrina and Rita and train derailments, caused prices to peak. The downward trend from the peak is primarily a result of regulatory uncertainty.

Use of This Asset Class as a Financing Mechanism

In addition to the relationship between price and technology decisions in the SO2 allowance spot prices, this market has a long-term price structure. On any given day, prices are available for a stream of future compliance years. This relationship is known as the forward curve. The first registered trade in the EPA was for a 30-year stream of allowances.

Figure 3.3. **Impact of Weather, Substitutes, and Regulations on SO2 Allowance Prices, 1994–2012**

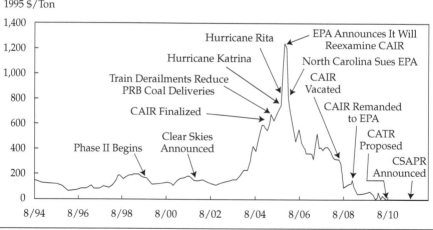

Note: PRB refers to Powder River Basin; CATR is the Clean Air Transport Rule.

Sources: Data on spot prices compiled by Power & Energy Analytic Resources from Cantor Fitzgerald until 11 September 2001 and from ICAP United thereafter.

Because scrubbers are expensive (costing up to $50 million or more), utilities borrow the money to install a scrubber and pay for it from future sales of emission allowances. The following example illustrates a financing approach that took price and technology factors into consideration. It also highlights the initial participation of financial players in the SO2 market in earlier years.

In 1993, Henderson Municipal Power & Light in Kentucky sold 150,000 tons of sulfur dioxide pollution allowances to Centre Financial Products (CFP), a boutique investment bank, for $26.8 million.[32] The sale of allowances represented the third-largest SO2 trade since 1992 (as of 1995). This was a unique sale because the revenue from the sale was used to finance and install scrubbers in the Station Two plant of Henderson Municipal, planned in April 1993. The scrubbers were estimated to cost $41 million. By installing these scrubbers, however, Henderson Municipal was able to decrease its sulfur emissions by 95%.[33] At the market price, the proceeds from the sale of allowances would be enough to finance the scrubbers.

In September 1993, CFP, in turn, sold the original 150,000 allowances to Carolina Power & Light (CP&L). CP&L used very low-sulfur coal in its generators. Thus, for it, the marginal cost of removing the remaining sulfur by a scrubber was higher than the industry average. In 1993, CP&L estimated this cost to be approximately $500 per ton of SO2. Comparatively, in March 1993, the EPA auctioned 150,010 allowances at the CBOT at an average price of $143. Furthermore, CP&L had little interest in installing scrubbing equipment at the time because scrubbing technology was still evolving.[34]

CP&L planned to introduce fuel switching and demand-side management to reduce emissions but, nonetheless, expected to exceed its EPA emission allotment. For the years from 2000 to 2009, the EPA allocated 143,968 allowances to CP&L per year. By CP&L estimates, if it failed to make any changes in the way it operated its system, it would emit approximately 230,000 tons of sulfur dioxide in the year 2000, creating a deficit of 86,000 tons. As a result, CP&L would have to reduce its SO2 emissions or purchase additional allowances.

CP&L first purchased 85,103 allowance credits at the 1993 EPA auction for $11,490,000, for an average price of $135 per credit. Requiring additional credits, the company entered into a formal agreement with CFP in 2000 for

---

[32]Clean Air Act Implementation: Hearings before the Subcommittee on Energy and Power of the Committee on Energy and Commerce, House of Representatives (29 September and 5 October 1994).

[33]Richard Sandor, *Good Derivatives: A Story of Financial and Environmental Innovation* (New York: John Wiley & Sons, 2012).

[34]State of North Carolina Utilities Commission–Raleigh, Docket No. E-2, Sub 642.

the purchase of 150,000 emission allowances for $47,250,000.[35] Using an 8% market interest rate over eight years, the discounted present value of that payment in 1993 was $27,560,000. CP&L needed to raise additional capital or borrow money to pay for the SO2 allowances, which posed a problem for CFP. Not only did CFP have to guarantee the interest rate for CP&L's capital increase, but it also had to guarantee the price and quantity of the allowances. To solve the first problem, CFP agreed to lend money to CP&L. Solving the second problem was more challenging. Because the EPA registry was not operational at the time the deal was consummated, CFP wrote the contract so that it would close when the registry was inaugurated.

Although the price and quantity of allowances were fixed through a forward purchase agreement with another utility, CFP still had to hedge against the interest rate risk. Because no futures market in corporate bonds existed, CFP had to use the US Treasury bond futures contract offered by the CBOT, which created basis risk. To mitigate this risk, CFP decided to also buy puts on the T-bond futures contract.

This last step was critical because CFP bought and sold the allowances at the same price. The profit came from the price at which CFP bought the debt from CP&L and then sold it to an insurance company. Interest rates fell between the time the contract was signed and the time the deal was closed. The structured transaction turned out to be very profitable in spite of the fact that CFP made little money on the purchase and sale of the allowances.

In the end, CP&L secured its future allowances at favorable prices and financed the transaction at attractive interest rates. The seller of the allowances (Henderson) also fared well. The sale and purchase were completed at a higher price than the OTC bid and a lower price than the OTC offer. This transaction seems simple, but a close examination reveals that the allowance market enabled not only a low-cost compliance tool but also a financing vehicle.

Investment Opportunities in This Asset Class

The constraints imposed by the SO2 cap-and-trade program also created opportunities. So far, we have focused on prices and allowances as an asset class, but other, related assets might be considered as investments.

Air Pollution Control. As previously mentioned, a major application for scrubbers is flue gas desulfurization (FGD), which constitutes a major share of the scrubbing business. Traditionally, FGD referred to wet scrubbers that remove SO2 emissions from large electric utility boilers used for coal combustion. FGD systems are being increasingly used, however, to remove

---

[35]"Execution of Proprietary Title IV Sulfur Dioxide Emission Allowances Purchase Agreement, Together with Note and Security Agreement," signed by Robert M. Williams.

SO2 emissions from process plants, including smelters, acid plants, refineries, and pulp and paper mills.

FGD scrubbing systems may be wet or dry. Wet scrubbers use liquid to remove particles or gases from exhaust systems. In contrast, dry scrubbers operate by spraying chemicals that neutralize flue gas and do not use a lot of water. Thus, dry scrubbing systems generally do not require wastewater management/treatment. Dry scrubbers are most commonly used to control SO2 and other acid gases from utility and industrial boilers and incinerators.[36]

For NOX at coal plants, selective catalytic reduction systems (SCRs) are installed at the plants. In an SCR, ammonia is injected, with the power plant flue gas, into a device that contains a catalyst to improve NOX removal efficiencies. According to the EPA, SCRs can achieve up to 90% NOX removal. SCRs in combination with SO2 scrubbers can also achieve up to 80% mercury removal.[37]

Today, with a significant number of units in the United States already having installed scrubbers and an increase in the use of natural gas, domestic opportunities in air pollution–control equipment are limited.[38] The next promising opportunities for pollution-control equipment are in Asia's emerging economies. Such countries as China and India are not only highly coal dependent in their generation of electricity but are also expecting further emissions-control policy mandates.

China has become the world's largest emitter of SO2. In 2010, absolute SO2 emissions in China approached 31 million tons, with approximately 66% coming from industry. For comparison, the United States had 5.17 million tons in 2010 of SO2 emissions (from electric power generation), which had been reduced from 17.5 million tons in 1980. China's government set a goal in the 11th Five-Year Plan (2006–2010) of a 10% reduction below 2005 levels of SO2 emissions by 2010. In the 12th Five-Year Plan, that goal became an 8% reduction for SO2 and a 10% reduction for NOX. Several pilot cap-and-trade programs for emissions reductions have built some knowledge of the

---

[36]US EPA, "Lesson 9: Flue Gas Desulfurization (Acid Gas Removal) Systems," US Environmental Protection Agency (2013): http://yosemite.epa.gov/oaqps/eogtrain.nsf/b81 bacb527b016d785256e4a004c0393/d4ec501f07c0e03a85256b6c006caf64/$FILE/si412c_lesson9.pdf. Accessed 2 May 2013.

[37]EPA, "IPM Analysis of the Final Mercury and Air Toxics Standards (MATS). Documentation: Updates to EPA Base Case v4.10_MATS," US EPA Clean Air Markets (December 2011): www.epa.gov/airmarket/progsregs/epa-ipm/toxics.html.

[38]Between 2007 and 2011, US coal-fired power plants invested more than $30 billion in FGD systems. Scrubbers were installed in about 110 coal-fired plants in 34 states during this time (around 60% of US coal-fired, steam electric generation capacity); see "U.S. Coal-Fired Power Plants Invested More than $30bn on Scrubbers in Four Years," *Power Engineering* (25 March 2013): www.power-eng.com/articles/2013/03/us-coal-fired-power-plants-invested-more-than-30bn-on-scrubbers-.html. Accessed 15 May 2013.

markets but have been less than distinguished in achieving reductions. China needs significantly greater rigor in its emissions monitoring and reporting as well as improved enforcement of emissions limits and allowance-holding requirements if the benefits of emissions markets are to be realized.

The social consequences of these emissions are devastating for China. The country currently has 16 of the 20 most polluted cities in the world. Some 500,000 people die prematurely from respiratory illnesses annually. Health care costs associated with air pollution amount to approximately 4% of China's gross domestic product (GDP). Furthermore, the environmental problems are not confined to China's borders. Japan and South Korea, in particular, have been adversely affected by acid rain. This pollution also travels across the Pacific Ocean and may be responsible for as much as 25% of particulate matter pollution in California on certain days.

A simple comparison might provide a sense of the magnitude of the challenge China faces in addressing the issue of acid rain. In the United States, the reduction of 9 million tons of SO2 was worth approximately $125 billion annually in reduced medical costs. Because China's current SO2 emissions are approximately 31 million tons (or six times the size of the US electric power industry's emissions) and China has approximately the same landmass as the United States but four times the population, a 9 million ton SO2 reduction could be four times more valuable in China, generating approximately $500 billion annually in reduced medical costs. Therefore, a SO2 emissions reduction of 18 million tons could avoid more than $1 trillion in contingent liability that hinders economic growth.

Even without mandates, power plants in East Asia will spend $4.8 billion on FGD this year, which represents 63% of the total worldwide expenditure. Including repair parts, upgrades, and such inputs as lime and limestone, total expenditures by the power sector for FGD in the world will exceed $15 billion in 2013.[39] The majority of the FGD sales in East Asia will be to power plants in China. Most of the sales in China will be to new power plants, but some retrofits to old power plants without FGD will take place. China has more scrubbers than any other country but also more power plants without scrubbers. China continues to spend more for new FGD systems than the rest of the world combined.[40]

---

[39]"East Asia Will Spend $4.8 Billion on FGD This Year," *Power Air Quality Insights*, no. 92 (31 January 2013): www.mcilvainecompany.com/Decision_Tree/subscriber/Tree/DescriptionTextLinks/Power%20Air%20Quality%20January%2031%202013.htm. Accessed 2 May 2013. The figure does not include repairs or such inputs as lime and limestone.

[40]China is the largest consumer of limestone and a leading producer of lime and limestone. It has a large lime reserve—190,000 metric tons as of 2010, according to the 2010 US Geological Survey, which is available at http://minerals.usgs.gov/minerals/pubs/country/2010/myb3-2010-ch.pdf. Accessed 2 May 2013.

The Financial Sector. As emissions markets mature, the growth of organized futures and options exchanges presents several opportunities for investors. Investors could gain exposure to the emissions marketplace by purchasing equity in specialized listed exchanges. Emitters/users can similarly gain access to this market by buying or selling SO2 spot and derivatives contracts and using the market for hedging purposes.

Exchanges offer enormous opportunities. Exchanges add value because they reduce the transaction costs of buying and selling allowances and make efficient risk transfer possible.[41] Opportunities also exist for financial players, such as investment banks, commercial banks, and brokers. Regulatory uncertainty in the United States suggests, however, that large financial institutions will play a diminished role in emissions markets. Evidence is the recent closing of trading desks by major investment banks.

The preceding discussion of the role of financial players and exchanges in the US Acid Rain Program could be informative for emerging economies that are contemplating establishing emissions markets. China and India, for example, have the potential to be large emissions markets. There could also be a role for commercial and investment banks and other market makers in jurisdictions where certain regulatory requirements on commercial and investment banks' trading activities are not in place. As was true in the United States, financial institutions play an important role in providing liquidity and efficiency to nascent markets.

Conclusion

Although the SO2 program is nominally still in place, the legal battles, regulatory uncertainty, and limitations on trading have virtually stalled market activity as of this writing. With regard to this particular pollutant, the United States has, in an ironic turn of events, turned its back on one of the most successful environmental programs ever put into place. Because of lack of congressional action and the DC Circuit Court's interpretation of the law, the United States has reverted to administrative solutions to climate change mitigation. This turn of events has resulted in largely bifurcated emissions markets and, therefore, limited options for utilities to reduce emissions.

The Acid Rain Program in the United States—specifically, its allowance-trading component—is a policy tool that proved to be successful from an economic and environmental standpoint. Despite regulatory setbacks, the Acid Rain Program built a track record that proves the system worked. Moreover, it helped build an institutional infrastructure in terms of compliance tools, monitoring, financial expertise, and technical expertise that are now about to

---

[41]Estimates suggest that transaction costs for compliance in the Acid Rain Program were reduced from $500 million to $20 million because of the existence of exchanges.

be emulated in other parts of the world. It opened financial possibilities for entrepreneurs and investors in exchanges, and pollution-control companies in the United States have expanded to carbon markets in other jurisdictions (see Chapter 4). Opportunities for market participants in the SO2 and NOX space will probably be present as emerging economies with serious pollution problems institute environmental regulations. That future will create further demand for these market participants' products, services, and ingenuity.

The Acid Rain Program also inspired the expansion of the cap-and-trade concept to deal with the perceived threat of climate change. In addition, it has been applied to Europe in the form of the European Union Emissions Trading Scheme.

4. Greenhouse Gas Pollutants as an Asset Class

Global warming has continued unabated since 1896 when Nobel Prize–winning Swedish scientist Svante Arrhenius first predicted it on the basis of increases in atmospheric CO_2. The pace of warming, measured through the concentration of CO_2 in the atmosphere rather than actual temperature, has increased from roughly 316 parts per million (ppm) in 1958 to about 400 ppm today.[42, 43]

Global warming can be the result of natural causes, such as the global water cycle, volcanic eruptions, or natural aerosols and biogenic emissions. But the evidence is strong that combustion of fossil fuels, commercial agriculture, deforestation, and other man-made causes related to industrialization have led to a rapid increase in CO_2, methane, and other greenhouse gas (GHG) emissions in the Earth's atmosphere—and thus to higher temperatures.[44] The effects are evident in the fact that the top 10 warmest years have all occurred since 1998; 2010 was the warmest year since the data began in 1880.

Our view is that the current debate about what causes global warming and political attitudes toward the subject are irrelevant and do not provide sufficient reason for inaction. From a purely risk management view, when opportunities exist to reduce the dangers of global warming that are cheaper than the catastrophic losses global warming may create, any and all options must be considered to combat it.[45]

Acid rain, our focus in Chapter 3, is primarily caused by SO2 and N_2O, but the phenomenon of global warming, on which we focus in this chapter, is caused by many pollutants.[46] Moreover, acid rain pollutants are regional pollutants; that is, their impact is generally restricted to the areas in which they

---

[42]The reference year 1958 is important because it denotes the first comprehensive measure of CO_2 levels in the atmosphere, by Charles Keeling from the Scripps Institution of Oceanography.

[43]Measuring the temperature of a whole planet is difficult, but sound theoretical reasons exist why the temperature of the Earth's surface should be related to atmospheric CO_2 concentration. See the Intergovernmental Panel on Climate Change: www.ipcc.ch.

[44]According to the Glossary of the UN Framework Convention on Climate Change, a GHG is any gas that absorbs infrared radiation in the atmosphere. See http://unfccc.int/resource/cd_roms/na1/ghg_inventories/english/8_glossary/Glossary.htm.

[45]This view is similar to those expressed by Richard A. Posner in *Catastrophe: Risk and Response* (Oxford, UK: Oxford University Press, 2004).

[46]GHGs include but are not limited to water vapor, carbon dioxide, methane, nitrous oxide, hydrochlorofluorocarbons, ozone, hydrofluorocarbons, perfluorocarbons, and sulfur hexafluoride.

are emitted (for example, the East Coast of the United States). Global warming is a much larger problem than acid rain because it is believed to be caused by an *overall* increase in the atmosphere's CO_2 concentration. The effects of global warming are multifold, and all countries are affected in one way or another. Global warming can cause climatic shocks, including variability in precipitation, flooding, changes in trade wind flows, and an increase in the intensity of extreme climate events, such as hurricanes. These events can have an economy-wide impact by affecting crop productivity, desertification (the degradation of arable land to desert), animal and human health, and sea levels. In addition, unlike acid rain, the effects of global warming are long term, so it truly is an intergenerational problem.

The policy responses to global warming include incentive schemes that shift demand away from fossil fuels and toward renewable energy and enhance fossil-fuel efficiencies. Examples of policy measures are direct subsidies to promote renewable energy, policy mandates requiring increased energy efficiency or that a certain percentage of power be generated from renewable sources, and preferential electricity tariffs for renewable energy generation.[47] In accordance with the previous discussion of acid rain, we will focus on the use of market-based mechanisms to reduce global warming—specifically, cap-and-trade.

The European Union Emissions Trading Scheme (EU ETS) is the largest and most successful implementation of the cap-and-trade model for GHGs. The EU ETS is a market for carbon permits among affected European companies within the 27 member states of the EU (the EU-27). Its goal is to achieve the GHG emissions-reduction goals agreed upon in the Kyoto Protocol, which will be discussed later, and reductions expected from future international agreements. So far, the EU ETS has enabled the EU-27 to successfully reduce its GHG emissions by 13% below its 1990 emissions levels. Currently, the EU ETS commands a market size in excess of $170 billion and accounts for nearly 75% of all international carbon trading.[48] The dynamics of the EU ETS are the principal drivers behind global carbon emissions markets today, and its success has led nations outside the EU to adopt a similar approach.

The purpose of this chapter is to use the EU ETS to demonstrate the role of cap-and-trade in reducing GHG emissions, a discussion that should be of interest to corporations, investors, and financial analysts. Under a cap-and-trade system limiting GHG emissions, corporations face new challenges and

---

[47]Preferential electricity tariffs are special (higher) rates provided as incentives to promote electricity generation from a certain source.

[48]The source for the market size data is "State and Trends of the Carbon Market 2012," Carbon Finance at the World Bank, Washington DC (May 2012): http://siteresources. worldbank.org/INTCARBONFINANCE/Resources/State_and_Trends_2012_Web_ Optimized_19035_Cvr&Txt_LR.pdf. Accessed 6 May 2013.

have to understand how to manage new risks and opportunities. Financial analysts need to understand the specific nature of carbon risk that corporations and their sectors are exposed to. In addition, analysts need to understand the new business challenges, commodity risks and opportunities, and, most importantly, trading opportunities that emerge as a result of emissions trading. Firms and entrepreneurs in finance, agribusiness, and industry have important investment opportunities in the sector. Climate change can affect the insurance industry, the health care industry, agricultural production, and resource scarcity. Quantifying and understanding the specific nature of climate change risk is crucial in asset management and portfolio allocation.

Several financial products have emerged because of the EU ETS. Moreover, emissions trading has provided new opportunities for financial institutions to create over-the-counter markets and new exchanges. New methods of financing, similar to those for SO2 allowances, have been created. This chapter provides the fundamentals to help the reader understand the drivers in asset classes related to global warming.

Global Warming: Causes and Public Policy Responses

Largely as a result of rapid industrialization, the concentration of GHG in the Earth's atmosphere has been steadily increasing since the Industrial Revolution. **Figure 4.1** shows that the rise in GHG concentrations closely correlates with the start of industrialization in the 19th century. In 1958, Charles Keeling, from the Scripps Institution of Oceanography, used scientific techniques to measure CO_2 levels in the Earth's atmosphere. The Keeling curve, presented in **Figure 4.2**, roughly matches the year-on-year increase in fossil-fuel combustion and helped to draw the world's attention to global warming. The Keeling curve in May 2013 showed that atmospheric concentration of CO_2 had reached 400 ppm, the highest level in at least three million years.[49] A large majority of scientists believe that the principal cause of this steady and alarming increase in atmospheric CO_2 levels is human activity (that is, the increase is "anthropogenic"). This is the focus of our discussion.

Historically, the developed nations in Europe and North America as well as Australia have been the primary contributors to GHG emissions. The United States was, until recently, the single largest contributor to GHG emissions, followed by the EU. Rapid industrialization in the developing world, however—dependent largely on the combustion of fossil fuels—is causing many developing countries to have high growth rates in emissions. In 2008,

---

[49]See the Intergovernmental Panel on Climate Change publications: www.ipcc.ch/publications_and_data/publications_and_data_reports.shtml#.UZUeZUqfVKI. Accessed 4 October 2013.

Figure 4.1. Historical GHG Concentrations

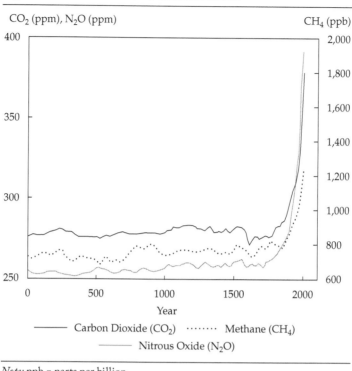

Note: ppb = parts per billion.

China emerged as the largest GHG emitter, with 6.5 billion metric tons of CO_2 per year.[50] India, the second most populous country, is also experiencing rapid increases in GHG emissions.

The sources for GHG emissions include electric utilities and manufacturing and industrial entities producing these pollutants from either fossil-fuel combustion or as by-products of chemical processing. The primary pollutant believed to cause global warming is carbon dioxide, which is largely emitted from the combustion of fossil fuels in electricity production, transportation, and manufacturing. Other contributors are methane released from landfills and agriculture (especially from the digestive systems of livestock), nitrogen oxide from fertilizers, gases used for refrigeration and industrial processes, and the loss of forests that would otherwise store CO_2. The primary GHGs and their designations are as follows:[51]

---

[50]UN ESCAP, *Statistical Yearbook for Asia and the Pacific 2011*, UN Economic and Social Commission for Asia and the Pacific: www.unescap.org/stat/data/syb2011/II-Environment/Air-pollution-and-climate-change.asp. Accessed 6 May 2013.

[51]Some of the designations are not precise chemical formulas but are in common use in the discussion of environmental finance and policy.

Figure 4.2. Keeling Curve Measuring Atmospheric CO$_2$ Levels, 1958–2013

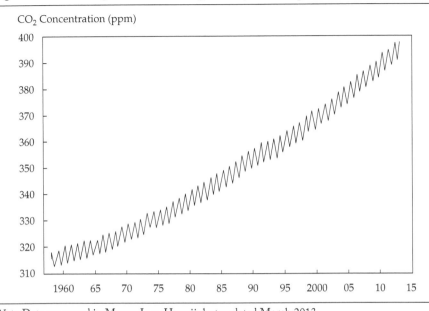

Note: Data measured in Mauna Loa, Hawaii; last updated March 2013.

- carbon dioxide (CO$_2$),

- methane (CH$_4$),

- nitrous oxide (N$_2$O),

- sulfur hexafluoride (SF$_6$),

- hydrofluorocarbons (HFCs), and

- perfluorocarbons (PFCs).

Each of the six GHGs has a different ability to trap heat, which is called its "global warming potential." For example, 1 ton of methane is roughly 26 times as potent as the equivalent amount of carbon dioxide. For the purposes of measurement relative to their global warming potential and the presentation of GHG emissions in standardized terms, emissions from all six gases are expressed in CO$_2$-equivalent terms. Appendix B provides an illustration of this mechanism and how it relates to emissions trading. The mechanics are shown to illustrate how the potential value of GHG reductions from various sources can have different impacts on supply and market price.

The policy response to climate change has largely been through the Kyoto Protocol of 1997, which had its genesis at the Earth Summit in Rio de Janeiro in 1992. The Earth Summit established the UN Framework Convention on Climate Change, which was the basis for the negotiation and agreement of the Kyoto Protocol. The Kyoto Protocol, ratified in 2004 (but not by the United States), limited GHG emissions to 5.2% below 1990 levels as an initial goal to be achieved between 2008 and 2012. The protocol included all six greenhouse gases and emissions from the industrial, electricity, and manufacturing sectors from 37 countries (most of which were developed) and set binding emissions targets. The signatory countries agreed to various national reduction targets based on historical emissions levels and stages of economic development. The Kyoto Protocol action to set the emissions baseline on the basis of historical emissions levels was similar to the process followed in the Acid Rain Program.

Importantly, the Kyoto Protocol provided several market-based avenues to meet the mandated national targets. The idea behind the Kyoto market mechanisms was to have flexibility in achieving each national target at the lowest costs with a goal of collectively achieving the overall GHG targets. These market mechanisms include (1) emissions trading; (2) a "clean development" mechanism, whereby developed countries can buy carbon allowances, called "Certified Emission Reductions" (CERs), that result from carbon-friendly investment in developing countries that lack GHG commitments; and (3) "joint implementation," whereby developed countries with binding emissions targets can earn emission-reduction units (ERUs) for investments among themselves in projects that reduce carbon emissions.

Under the Kyoto Protocol, the EU as a whole had a reduction target of 8% below 1990 levels. The EU shared this burden: Its members reallocated their Kyoto emission-reduction commitments among themselves and launched their own initially CO_2-focused program, the EU Emissions Trading Scheme (EU ETS), as the centerpiece of the climate policy. Therefore, some countries had steep targets whereas others had much more gradual emission-reduction slopes. Still others were allowed to increase their emissions. For example, Germany and Austria agreed to reduce their emissions to levels 21% and 13% below 1990 levels, respectively, whereas Ireland and Greece were allowed to increase their emissions by 13% above 1990 levels.[52] Finland and France were required to keep their emissions stable at 1990 levels. The purpose of this "bubble" within the Kyoto Protocol was to assist the EU in reaching its overall Kyoto target of 8% "with the least possible diminution of economic development and employment."[53] The core elements of the EU ETS were set

[52]Average 2008–11 emissions in Ireland were 11.5% higher than the base-year level but below the burden-sharing target of 13% for the period 2008–2012. See www.eea.europa.eu/publications/ghg-trends-and-projections-2012.
[53]European Council, "Greenhouse Gas Emission Allowance Trading Scheme," Directive 2003/87/EC of the European Parliament and of the Council of 13 October 2003: http://europa.eu/legislation_summaries/energy/european_energy_policy/l28012_en.htm.

out in a directive issued by the European Commission on 23 October 2003. Policymakers from other nations with large emissions, such as China and India, can learn from the EU model on the applicability of achieving national GHG targets by using "bubbles" among their states and provinces.

The EU ETS was implemented in three phases:

I. An initial pilot, often referred to as EU ETS Phase I, operated from 2005 to 2007.

II. EU ETS Phase II operated from 2008 to 2012 to achieve the agreed Kyoto reductions over that period.

III. EU ETS Phase III operates currently—that is, from 2013 through 2020.

These phases are discussed in detail later in this chapter.

With this background on the Kyoto mechanisms provided, we turn in the next section to the results of the EU ETS.

Results of the Public Policy Responses

The EU ETS more than achieved its established environmental goal, and strong reasons exist to believe it was accomplished with the least cost to society that was practical. This outcome was facilitated by the cap-and-trade market mechanism, which allowed flexibility in achieving emissions targets by establishing a price for emissions. Like the Acid Rain Program, the EU ETS—by setting a price for pollution, establishing a reduction target, and allowing flexibility in achieving the goal—proved that the cap-and-trade model can work even in the case of a multinational effort to manage a multi-source global pollutant.

From an environmental standpoint, the program has delivered significant emission reductions between its inception in 2005 and its third phase. The European Environmental Agency states not only that the mandated EU-15 (the 15 countries that were EU members as of the 2004 enlargement) are on track to meet their 8% reduction target but also that they have over-achieved the target by 4.9%, or 211 million metric tons per year. A Center for European Policy Studies (CEPS) study confirms that the EU ETS drove down emissions in Phase II beyond levels that could have been caused by the economic recession that struck in late 2008.[54] These studies use EU-wide emissions and EU ETS sectoral emissions data, together with economic data, to point out that the reductions were achieved at the same time as significant improvements in *emission intensity* (which refers to the amount of emissions

---

[54]Anton Georgiev, Monica Alessi, Christian Egenhofer, and Noriko Fujiwara, "The EU Emissions Trading System and Climate Policy towards 2050: Real Incentives to Reduce Emissions and Drive Innovation?" *CEPS Special Reports* and *Climate Change* (January 2011).

per unit of production or GDP). Other estimates of the specific role the EU ETS played in EU emission reductions indicate that it accounted for about 40% of the 3% EU emission reduction achieved in 2008 alone.[55] In addition, these observed reduction trends are continuing well beyond 2008.

Note that EU emission reductions have been achieved even as GDP has increased, which suggests that low-carbon economic growth is feasible. The EU economic numbers suggest that, although the output of the EU economy has recovered to about the 2007 level, emissions are significantly lower than in 2007. Compared with 1990 levels, EU-27 emissions are 17% lower, even though GDP grew by more than 40% and manufacturing by more than 12%. With regard to the impact on competitiveness, a 2011 study summarizing published literature and data from more than 2,000 European firms covered by the ETS[56] concluded that the program did not significantly affect profits, employment, or added value, despite concerns expressed by some affected firms and sectors.

The EU Emissions Trading Scheme

The fundamental structure and operational mechanism for the EU ETS mirror the Acid Rain Program. The EU ETS operates through the allocation and trading of GHG allowances, the EU Allowances (EUAs). Each EUA represents 1 ton of carbon dioxide or its equivalent, and the EUA is the EU emissions-trading unit.

The EUAs are held as serialized electronic records within an electronic registry operated and overseen by the European Commission. These web-accessible registry systems contain and track transfers of the issued EUAs, including those held by nonemitting entities (and individuals) that wish to participate in trading. The registry system can also be used for tracking and monitoring the binding compliance targets for mandated entities and installations within the EU. At the end of each year, the European Commission matches the actual emissions of regulated entities with their surrendered EUAs. Noncompliance leads to a penalty of €100 per ton in addition to making entities surrender the required allowances to meet compliance.

Recall that the same model was applied for SO2. In fact, even the term "allowance" was borrowed from the Acid Rain Program.

However, some points of divergence between the operational setup of the Acid Rain Program and that of the EU ETS are worth noting.

---

[55]"Emissions from EU ETS Down 3% in 2008," press release, New Carbon Finance (16 February 2009).
[56]Anton Georgiev, Monica Alessi, Christian Egenhofer, Noriko Fujiwara, "The EU Emissions Trading System and Climate Policy towards 2050: Real Incentives to Reduce Emissions and Drive Innovation?" *CEPS Special Reports* (January 2011).

Specifically, individual EU member states developed their own national EUA registries. These registries were then interlinked in an EU-wide network to facilitate transfer among the various registries. This model differs from the Acid Rain Program model, where a single centralized registry managed allowance transfers.

The creation of multiple registries was a complex undertaking and created some operational inefficiencies and delays in the early days of the EU ETS. In the initial days, national registries also reflected some sovereign risks that do not exist for a single-nation centralized registry. In the later days of the EU ETS, some fraudulent transactions and allowance theft took place that perhaps could have been avoided with a single-registry system.

The EU ETS is a far more complex system than the Acid Rain Program. It involves many nations, multiple gases from diverse sectors versus two gases largely from electricity generators, and implementation through international agreements versus national environmental directives.

Implementation Schedule. This subsection begins with salient aspects of Phase I of the program and then focuses largely on Phase II and beyond.

▨ *Phase I.* Phase I of the EU ETS began in 2005, three years ahead of the first Kyoto commitment period. Phase I was intended to be a "learning-by-doing" phase to initiate the process of capacity building and infrastructure establishment in preparation for the Kyoto commitments. Phase I was confined to carbon dioxide emissions, and the EU-wide total allocation of emission allowances was approximately 2.1 billion metric tons of CO_2 per year.

As intended, Phase I involved much learning by both regulators and market participants. Much of the institution building, including the hardware setup for allowance trading, was established in this phase. The price movement in this phase reflected several uncertainties in a developing marketplace. In the early periods of Phase I, regulatory uncertainties surrounding allowance allocations by participating EU nations and Russia's ratification were the primary sources of price risk. Two design flaws in Phase I stand out, however, and deserve further description.

First, verified EU emission reductions in early 2006 revealed that the EU had overallocated emission allowances. When developing Phase I, the EU lacked reliable emissions data for specific industries and corporations for prior years. The EU allowed member countries to allocate allowances on the basis of polluters' own estimates of emissions rather than verified data of historical emissions. This oversight resulted in member countries applying their own rules for national allowance allocations and issuing allowances on the basis of optimistic (low) forecasts of emissions growth.

This practice represents a major departure from the Acid Rain Program, in which facilities were allocated allowances on the basis of historical emissions from individual electricity-generating units. The Acid Rain Program teaches us that sound measurement and emissions monitoring are critical in building a viable emissions market.

Another controversial issue related to the allowance allocation was that allowances were issued free of cost. Some critics pointed out that such allowance allocation led to windfall profits, particularly in the partially deregulated power sector.[57] One such analysis estimated that windfall profits for the power sector were on the order of $16.6 billion for Phase I.[58] Note, however, that these problems were not EU wide and varied from country to country. In all, the oversupply of allowances resulted in EU ETS Phase I allowance prices falling dramatically in early 2006.

In the later part of Phase I, the allowance price fell close to zero. This outcome reveals the second flaw, a structural fault in the design. In designing the market framework for the EU ETS, banking or borrowing of EUAs between Phase I (2005–2007) and Phase II (2007–2012) of the program was not allowed. In addition, uncertainty about whether this provision would be implemented affected market decisions and price volatility. By rule, EU ETS Phase I allowances remaining in registry accounts were to be cancelled at the end of the program. As expected, any unused Phase I allowances held by affected entities became worthless at that time.

Management of the release of price-sensitive information could also have been better. The price decline accelerated toward the end because Phase I entities with surplus allowances sold whatever inventory remained of the allowances. Combined with the fact that EU ETS Phase I was already overallocated, the price of Phase I allowances fell drastically toward the end of the phase, as depicted in **Figure 4.3**.

The trading and market-making community responded to these expected price movements and profited from the arbitrage opportunities. One astute trading strategy involved shorting the 2007 allowance contract and going long the 2008 allowance contract. The trade worked because overallocation and the absence of a banking provision caused the 2007 allowance price to fall to zero, whereas those problems did not apply to the 2008 allowances.

▪ *Phase II.* This phase ran from January 2008 through December 2012 and coincided with the first commitment period in the Kyoto Protocol, which included all six of the greenhouse gases recognized under Kyoto (although the EU ETS still focused on CO_2) and intended to reduce their emissions

---

[57]The allegation was that windfall profits occurred when the deregulated power sector was able to pass on the cost of allowances to consumers, although it received the allowance for free.

[58]A. Denny Ellerman, Frank J. Convery, and Christian de Perthuis, *Pricing Carbon: The European Union Emissions Trading Scheme* (Cambridge, UK: Cambridge University Press, 2010).

Figure 4.3. Historical EUA Price and Price Drivers, 2005–2013

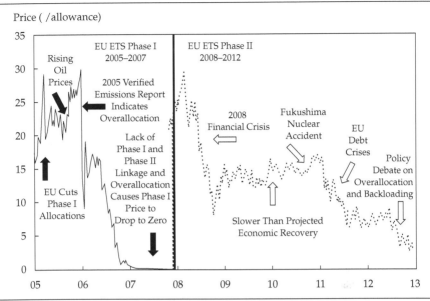

Source: European Environment Agency Data and Maps: www.eea.europa.eu/data-and-maps. Accessed 4 October 2013.

to a level 8% below 1990 levels. In July 2003, the EU further adopted a proposal to link offsets from the clean development mechanism (CDM) and joint implementation (JI) with Phase II and subsequent phases of EU ETS. Under the directive, European emitters are allowed to supplement their carbon-mitigation measures with offsets earned from CDM and JI projects, up to specified limits. The directive stated that the purpose of the link was to achieve cost-effectiveness in reducing global GHG emissions and increased liquidity by introducing diverse low-cost compliance options.

■ *Phase III.* The EU ETS is now in its third phase, which will run from 2012 through 2020. Phase III covers roughly 45% of total EU CO_2 emissions and more than 11,000 power stations and manufacturing plants in 31 nations in Europe.[59] Covered emissions include those from power stations and other combustion plants; oil refineries; coke ovens; iron and steel plants; and the cement, glass, lime, bricks, ceramics, and pulp, paper, and board sectors. Furthermore, Phase III includes a separate emissions-trading program intended to reduce CO_2 emissions from the aviation sector. The emissions reduction in this phase is 1.74% per year, which means that by the end of Phase III in 2020, EU-wide GHG emissions should be 21% lower than in 2005.

[59]Countries of the EU ETS are the EU-27 plus Croatia, Iceland, Liechtenstein, and Norway.

The fourth trading period is expected to run from 2021 to 2028. **Figure 4.4** shows the EU emissions caps for various phases of the program.

Market Size. With an annual allowance allocation of **approximately 2 billion EUAs** and an assumed price of $6 per allowance, the total notional value of the EUA market is about $12.8 billion. The traded volumes of the EUAs far exceed the annual allocations, however, which indicates a market size that is several times larger. Part of the reason is that trading includes forward transactions for compliance in future years as well as trading by portfolio investors, market makers, and speculators. Thus, the secondary market is maturing. In 2011, a total of 7.9 billion EUAs were traded, representing a value of $148.8 billion.

To put this amount in perspective, consider that the 2011 value of the "carbon crop" exceeded the production value of all US corn, wheat, and soybeans for the same year.[60] **Figure 4.5** presents the historical growth in the EU ETS market from 2006 to 2011. Relative to the allocation, the traded volume of allowances has increased substantially. Since 2008, the markets have turned over more than the annual allocation of allowances each year.

---

[60]The USDA crop value of production for corn for grain was $76.9 billion; wheat, $14.3 billion; and soybeans, $38.5 billion (National Agricultural Statistics Service, US Department of Agriculture).

Figure 4.4. The EU ETS Cap in Various Phases, 2005–2050

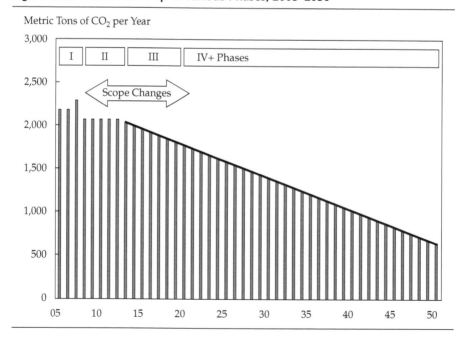

Metric Tons of CO_2 per Year

Figure 4.5   EU ETS Market Statistics, 2006–2011

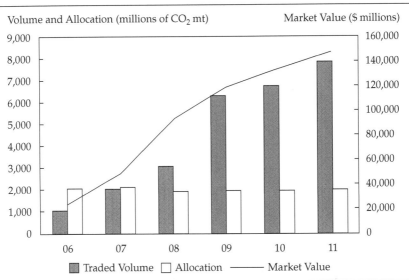

Volume and Allocation (millions of CO_2 mt)   Market Value ($ millions)

Notes: Data are for European Union Allowances. Allocation refers to the initial allocation of EUAs to entities in the EU mandated to reduce their emissions. Traded Volume refers to the quantity of EUAs traded in a year. Market Value refers to the product of market price and quantity traded in a given year. mt = metric tons.

One of the signals for a maturing market used by the derivatives industry is an increasing "churn" rate. EU ETS churn rates in 2011 were close to four times the allowance allocation.

The EU ETS market is liquid, which is essential for reducing transaction costs and improving market efficiencies. Organized exchanges create economic value by narrowing the bid–ask spread and through price transparency. To illustrate, note that the initial bid–ask spread in the EU ETS was €0.20–€0.25. By the end of 2010, this spread had narrowed to €0.02, generating more than €1 billion in savings for the EU.

Trading in EUAs takes place through various avenues, including bilateral transactions, spot markets, and futures and options markets. About 10 regulated commodity futures exchanges provide hedging products for managing risks from EU ETS. The smallest segment is the spot market, with $2.8 billion in transaction value and representing about 2% of total EU transaction volume. EUA futures, with $130.8 billion in value and more than 88% of all EUA transactions, represent the largest segment. The options market, at about $14.2 billion, represents 10% of the EUA transaction volumes.

The CER and ERU markets are much smaller than the EUA market. In 2011, the combined value of CER and ERU transactions was only about

$23 billion, representing a volume of about 1.8 billion allowances. Trading in CERs represented 97% of the transaction value. Following a trading pattern similar to that of the EUA, the vast majority (92%) of the traded volume in CERs and ERUs was done with futures and options instruments. The transaction volume and value of the various instruments are shown in **Table 4.1.**

Price History. Early estimates for EU ETS Phase II allowance prices were not only optimistic but also predicated on an increase in the allowance price over time. The price expectations for EUAs and the actual market prices show a remarkable similarity with the SO2 allowance market. **Table 4.2** gives a range of price forecasts for Phase II allowances from various studies. In reality, the actual price for EUAs between 2008 and 2013 has largely been below the optimistic forecasts. From an investment standpoint in early 2009, comparing these predictions with actual EUA prices would suggest that buying allowances was a good investment opportunity. The history of EUA prices indicates, however, that a decision to hold a long position in allowances would have been incorrect. Figure 4.3 shows the major factors that triggered price movements.

Clearly, early predictions of EUA prices were factoring in some high-cost technological solutions. Technological solutions available to power plants included emerging carbon capture and storage, which becomes feasible in

Table 4.1. Composition of the Greenhouse Gas Market in 2011

	Transaction Volume ($MtCO_2e$)	Transaction Value ($ millions)
EUA	7,853	$147,848
CER	1,734	22,333
ERU	76	780
Total	9,663	$170,961

Note: $MtCO_2e$ = million metric tons of carbon dioxide equivalent.

Table 4.2. EUA Allowance Price Forecasts

Source	Range
Industry survey by Point Carbon (June 2007)	$30–$35 per allowance
Industry survey by Point Carbon (October 2008)	$30–$45 per allowance
Deutsche Bank (2007)	$35 per allowance
Société Générale (2010)	$22–$60 per allowance
Trend of price forecast for European allowances[a]	$15.5–$33.6 per allowance

[a]M. Prada, J.J. Barbéris, and A. Tignol, "La Régulation des Marchés du CO_2," Ministere de L'Ecologie, République Française, Mongraphie 18730 (2010).

the range of \$30–\$55 per allowance.[61] Similarly, alternative fuel technologies, such as solar photovoltaic and concentrated solar power, are economically viable when allowance prices are higher than \$28 per ton. In Europe, a recent report states that allowance prices of \$35–\$40 are needed to switch from burning highly polluting coal to natural gas. Société Générale estimates that utilities will invest in clean technology at an EUA price on the order of €30 per ton.

As with the Acid Rain Program, a combination of factors determined EUA prices. In addition to the technological alternatives that allowed companies to achieve reductions, such as fuel switching and improvements in energy efficiency, an important factor was the so-called banking provisions. These provisions allowed entities to manage their EUA requirements over time and thereby kept prices stable. (This method was also frequently used in the Acid Rain Program, as noted in Chapter 3.) Other price determinants in the EU ETS involved economic shocks and regulatory policy uncertainties. These developments are discussed here.

First, the worldwide 2008 financial crisis was a significant economic shock that reduced industrial production globally, thereby curbing emissions. The price of EUAs fell to less than €15 per ton. Following the economic crisis, the EUA price remained depressed because European economic growth was slower than expected.

Second, and more recently, Europe was hit by a severe government debt crisis. EUA prices fell in 2011 to below €10 per ton and continued to fall in 2012.

Sadly, much as proved true with the Acid Rain Program, the biggest shock to the EUA emissions market turned out to be sovereign risk. Keep in mind that the emissions allowance market exists largely as a result of a mandated cap by a regulatory authority. The European carbon market is currently witnessing a substantial oversupply of credits because of various factors. Estimates of oversupply are in the range of 1.4 billion tons for the phase until 2020. The EU, reeling from low economic growth, the debt crisis, and government austerity measures, has so far not reached a consensus on dealing

---

[61]McKinsey & Company, "Pathways to a Low-Carbon Economy," McKinsey & Company (January 2009): https://solutions.mckinsey.com/climatedesk/default.aspx. Accessed 4 October 2013. L.M. Abadie and J.M. Chamorro, "European CO_2 Prices and Carbon Capture Investments," *Energy Economics*, vol. 30, no. 6 (November 2008):2992–3015. R.G. Newell, A.B. Jaffe, and R.N. Stavin, "The Effects of Economic and Policy Incentives on Carbon Mitigation Technologies," *Energy Economics*, vol. 28, no. 5–6 (November 2006):563–578. R.C. Sekar, J.E. Parsons, H.J. Herzog, and H.D. Jacoby, "Future Carbon Regulations and Current Investments in Alternative Coal-Fired Power Plant Technologies," *Economic Policy*, vol. 35 (2007):1064–1074. D. Martinsen, J. Linssen, P. Markewitz, and S. Vögele, "CCS: A Future CO_2 Mitigation Option for Germany? A Bottom-Up Approach," *Energy Policy*, vol. 35, no. 4 (April 2007):2110–2120.

with the oversupply. Industry analysts suggest that EUA prices could remain depressed in the medium and perhaps long term as a result of sovereign risk. In retrospect, EUA market prices indicate that, in light of such shocks, investors should have sold allowances short.

The EUA market became further depressed because of delays and/or the lack of a policy to tackle the overallocation of EUAs in the market. Although more than the required emission reductions have been achieved in a cost-efficient manner, the EU is considering a determination, called "backloading," to restrict excess allowances in an effort to slow the price decline. Lack of consensus on this issue has led to EUA prices falling below €5 as of this writing. We believe that the best way to manage this problem is to focus on further emission-reduction goals.

Where changing the reduction target is not politically feasible, a price floor has been implemented. This mechanism is in place for California cap-and-trade and the Regional Greenhouse Gas Initiative program, which will be discussed in later sections of this chapter.

Price Determinants. In monitoring and analyzing market and price developments, financial analysts need to understand how these drivers interact, which drivers carry the most market weight, and, last but not least, to what extent and in what circumstances various drivers affect allowance prices. Entities affected by EU ETS exposure have to be informed about their trading and risk management, investment decisions, and abatement options. These decisions span a wide range of expertise germane to the technical, managerial, financial, and legal issues arising from the EU ETS.

EU ETS emissions allowance prices can be subject to two sets of factors: (1) long-run, systemic factors, such as policy and regulatory developments, advances in emission-reduction technology, and taxation and accounting issues, and (2) energy market developments, such as electricity transmission issues (new lines, regulations mandating open access). Energy market developments can influence not only electricity production levels but also emissions prices. Long-term developments that affect access to coal use, such as coal transportation infrastructure and pricing, can change the economics of coal selection and thereby influence emissions levels. As in the case of most commodities, also important are long-term macroeconomic variables, such as population growth, demographics, and natural resource scarcity, all of which influence prices.

Short-term fluctuations in the consumption of GHG emission allowances are influenced by, among other things, factors that affect electricity production and the composition of electricity production. Electricity production is influenced by economic activity, particularly industrial production, and by weather conditions (often measured by heating- and cooling-degree days). The composition of electricity production—in particular, the share of total production coming from fossil-fuel plants—is influenced by the availability of nuclear power, renewable energy, hydroelectric generation resources, and prices of substitute lower-emitting fuels, each of which may be affected by government support and other policies.

Many of the market drivers that affect the SO2 allowance market also affect the GHG allowance market because the majority of GHG emissions arise from combustion of fossil fuels that are also implicated in SO2 emissions. Rather than discuss those drivers again, we will focus on the drivers unique to GHG in this section.

Technological Options. The primary options are fuel switching and energy efficiency, although some other options are possible.

▨ *Fuel switching.* Similar to the examples noted for acid rain, fuel switching was a major avenue used by emitters to meet EU ETS compliance targets. Studies suggest that 80% of the abatement occurred in the EU-15, with the bulk of it in the energy sector. Here, the abatements were driven primarily by converting from coal to natural gas (fuel switching) as a direct result of either the observed or the expected carbon price.[62] Fuel switching in the power sector alone in Phase I contributed between 53 million and 98 million tons of reductions.[63] The Spanish utility Iberdrola reported switching 63% of its coal-fired generation to natural gas and increasing its natural gas generation by 52% in the first three quarters of 2008.[64] Similarly, Unión Fenosa, another Spanish utility, reduced coal-fired generation by 42% and increased gas-fired generation by 38% in the first half of 2008.[65] Spanish electricity-sector emissions of CO_2 went down in 2008 in spite of increases in net generation. This development is a good signal that economic growth and the transition to low carbon can be done in parallel.

The trends observed in the power sector were true also for the industrial sector. In 2006, SABMiller, the multinational brewing and beverage company headquartered in London, used fuel switching in its breweries and achieved a 12% improvement (decrease) in carbon intensity.[66]

▨ *Energy efficiency.* Another avenue in the power sector was to upgrade power plant efficiencies. Drax Group, a large coal-fired plant in the United

---

[62]Ellerman et al., *Pricing Carbon*, op cit.

[63]Note, however, that even though Phase I was a warm-up phase, companies planned ahead for the tighter restrictions to come in Phase II. Thus, they invested in the best methods to comply with future regulations.

[64]"Spanish Utility Iberdrola Cuts Carbon Emissions," Point Carbon (23 October 2008).

[65]"Union Fenosa Switches from Coal to Gas," Point Carbon (16 July 2008).

[66]"SAB Miller Cuts Carbon Intensity 12% in 2006," Point Carbon (4 July 2007).

Kingdom and one of the top five emitting sources in Europe, used this strategy. In response to the EU ETS, in 2007 the company invested about £100 million in upgrading its turbines and another £80 million to increase its renewable biomass co-firing facility fivefold. These measures combined resulted in a 15% reduction in emissions in the plant and, in addition, generated renewable energy certificates (RECs) that could be monetized. Financial analysts must note that the payback in this investment was from fuel savings as well as RECs.

Another utility, CEZ Group in the Czech Republic, implemented a range of efficiency measures, such as reconstructing feeding pumps, cooling pumps, and boilers and replacing turbines. These upgrades had been in the works but were implemented sooner than planned. They cost CEZ an additional €21 million in 2005,[67] but by selling the EUAs saved by the project, CEZ ended up recouping these costs and earning a profit of €7.7 million. RWE in Germany responded to the EU ETS by increasing its R&D investments in energy efficiency and fossil-fuel emission-reduction technologies by almost 32%.[68] Other utilities did the same. Planned 800 megawatt coal-fired plants in Poland, to be constructed by 2015 by RWE and the Polish utility Kompania Weglowa, are expected to have an efficiency of about 46% as opposed to the reference level of 33% in Polish coal-fired plants.[69, 70]

▧ *Other technological avenues.* The EU ETS experience included industry-specific avenues for emissions abatement. For example, the manufacture of blended cement, which involves partial substitution of such additives as fly ash for CO_2-intensive clinker in the cement industry, resulted in significant reductions in emissions.[71] Although the choice of blended cement cannot be attributed only to the ETS, its manufacture did have an impact on ETS compliance. CEMEX UK's 1.2 million ton blended-cement facility in Essex will cut CO_2 emissions in half by using such substitutes as fly ash for clinker. Studies have also suggested that the EU ETS triggered behavioral changes among managers by encouraging investment in energy efficiency, with the biggest gains resulting from large investments.

At present, a method that is technologically and economically viable to remove GHGs—comparable to the SO2 scrubbing technologies—does not exist. The closest alternative in the power sector is the use of carbon capture and storage (CCS) technologies, which can have a significant impact

---

[67]Ellerman et al., *Pricing Carbon*, op cit.

[68]"EUA Cost RWE €1 Billion in Jan–Sept 2008," Point Carbon (4 July 2007).

[69]"RWE to Build New Coal Plant in Poland," Point Carbon (4 July 2007).

[70]Efficiency in this context is defined as the ability to generate more electricity from the same quantity of coal combustion.

[71]Clinker is small lumps or nodules, usually from limestone, that are ground to produce cements. It is a heavily CO_2-intensive input in cement manufacture.

on emission reductions. CCS involves capturing the CO_2 produced by large combustion plants, compressing it for transportation, and then injecting it deep into a rock formation at a carefully selected and safe site, where it is permanently stored. CCS technologies are still in the early stages of development, however, and are not economically viable at current prices of carbon.

Regulatory Issues. The biggest factor affecting all cap-and-trade markets is the policy and regulatory framework because these markets are created either through political decisions framed in law or by means of caps imposed by some form of public or private contract. Hence, changes in laws, regulations, and operating guidelines can have a significant impact on market and price developments. In addition, regulation of, or taxation guidance on, the treatment of allowance transactions (including issuance, sales, purchases, swaps, and so on) for value-added taxes and financial accounting may influence trading and, therefore, prices. Anyone aiming to analyze and forecast market and price developments thus needs to understand the role and potential impact of policy choices.

▓ *Banking and borrowing provisions.* An important flexibility provision in emissions-trading systems is the ability of companies to transfer or bank any surplus allowances from one compliance period to use in future compliance periods. This option helps companies with the intertemporal risk management of their carbon exposure. For example, companies that have surplus emission allowances and expect that the demand for allowances will increase (either externally in the market or internally for their own future compliance) can bank these allowances for future years. Conversely, because in many cases allowances for the entire commitment period are issued in advance, companies can borrow from future years for current compliance. The option of borrowing can be seen as a relief valve for companies, to the extent that extreme weather conditions may have a large impact on the allowance balance for a single year. Limited or no banking or borrowing provisions would leave allowance prices largely determined by the need to comply fully in each period, which could affect short-term fundamentals and increase market volatility without necessarily improving long-term environmental compliance.

As shown in Chapter 3, the Acid Rain Program allowed for banking of allowances for use in future years. This provision allowed power plants to manage their compliance needs over time and played a role in maintaining price stability in the initial phases of the SO2 program. The EU ETS story demonstrates the adverse outcome that may result from not having this policy. As discussed, the lack of banking allowances between Phases I and II of the EU ETS (justified by an unwillingness of policymakers to create a bridge between the learning-by-doing phase and the period of Kyoto obligations) was a major reason for the decrease of Phase I prices to zero.

Regulatory Uncertainty. A lack of policy certainty regarding the rules governing an emissions-trading program has had major effects on allowance prices. In the EU ETS, numerous regulatory shocks—including uncertainties about the overall reduction goals, intermediate emission targets, quantity and method of allocation, provisions for banking or use of past allowances in future years, rules governing linking of the market with other programs, and the future status of the program—affected allowance prices.

Examples of regulatory influences on EU ETS prices are numerous. In the early days of the program, considerable uncertainty surrounded the aggregate national allowance allocations and the share of allowances to be allocated to each industrial sector within individual EU members. Naturally, this uncertainty had a higher impact in large EU economies that depended on coal-generated power, such as Germany. Recently, the debate on an appropriate mechanism to manage low EUA prices, such as backloading EUAs, has become a cause of price volatility. Market participants would be well advised to stay informed about these developments.

Offset Potential. Carbon and greenhouse gases are unique among atmospheric pollutants in that several sources create and mitigate them. A wide variety of CO_2-absorbing sinks and GHG-destruction technologies act as offsetting avenues to GHG emissions.[72] This situation led to the development of an offset market in which offset allowances generated from GHG-reducing projects are used, within regulatory limits, to meet compliance targets. Examples of technologies for sourcing offsets include energy efficiency, renewable energy (wind, hydro, and biomass), changes in industrial processes, and methane destruction from animal manure, among others. (Offset opportunities did not exist for acid rain pollutants.)

The EU ETS did not allow for offset credits to be generated internally within the EU. The program did, however, allow for the use of Kyoto compliance instruments, such as Certified Emission Reductions for compliance in the EU ETS. CERs, a type of carbon allowance or credit, were meant to assist developing countries in achieving sustainable development and contribute to the ultimate goal of stabilizing GHG concentrations in the atmosphere. In theory, EUA prices can be affected by CER supply and other regulatory issues. In reality, however, EUA pricing remained unaffected by the CER link in the EU ETS. CERs were not used in Phase I because not many were actually issued until 2008. In Phase II, the EU imposed an explicit annual cap

---

[72]A carbon sink is a natural or artificial reservoir that accumulates and stores some carbon-containing chemical compound for an indefinite period.

(13.4% of total CERs outstanding) on the proportion of CERs that could be used for compliance. Also, some sovereign risk was embedded in the CERs, depending on the country of origin and type. Given these factors, the link did not significantly affect EUA prices.

Carbon as Innovation Catalyst in Europe

As a direct result of the EU ETS, several innovative technologies were deployed in the EU. In some cases, these technologies generated new products and new revenue streams for the companies that produced them. Three examples of such innovative approaches are presented here.

Example 1. Fuel Switching in the Paper and Pulp Industry. The paper and pulp industry is a significant contributor to GHG emissions. This sector covers about 7% of mandated entities under the EU ETS. The EU ETS was a key reason for reducing emissions and energy use in Sweden's paper and pulp industry. Estimates suggest that improvements in energy use and fuel switching in that sector have led to emission reductions worth $12 million to $35 million annually in Sweden alone.

Sweden's Södra Cell Värö pulp mill has been successful in fully switching all of its fossil-fuel energy sources to carbon-neutral sources. Specifically, to generate steam, the paper mill uses a by-product from the digestion of pulpwood called "black liquor," together with waste bark. These biofuels generate 99% of the mill's power. The mill also exports nearly 65 gigawatts of electricity to the electric grid and provides energy to meet nearly half of the heating needs of a nearby town.

Chemrec, another Swedish paper and pulp company, has gone further with its black liquor. The company produces renewable motor fuels and electricity with this industrial by-product. Chemrec claims its black liquor motor fuel can satisfy the energy needs of up to half of Sweden's trucks. This example illustrates how innovative companies have used the EU ETS not only to transform their own energy use but also to develop additional products and business streams that add to their bottom line.

Example 2. Carbon Dioxide Fertilization for Horticulture. Carbon dioxide is an important energy source for plants, and CO_2 fertilization has important applications in agriculture. Royal Dutch Shell's refineries have creatively used CO_2 emissions from smokestacks to promote commercial horticulture in the Netherlands.

Shell's oil refinery in Rotterdam is the largest refinery in Europe. It emits about 6 million tons of CO_2 annually and accounts for nearly 3% of the Netherlands' GHG emissions. This unit captures about 350,000 tons of CO_2 from its smokestacks and uses it to fertilize 500 large greenhouses for horticulture. The recycled CO_2 is used as a substitute for about 95 million cubic meters of natural gas that otherwise would have been used annually for heating the greenhouses. This technology is not new, but it was economically feasible only because of the carbon price imposed by the EU ETS. For Shell, redirecting its smokestack emissions means capturing surplus EUAs, and for greenhouse operators, it means savings in heat used. This trade is a win–win situation for both Shell and the greenhouse operator and is in operation even though ETS rules affecting the project have changed.

Example 3. Use of Waste Heat for Energy. A by-product of fossil-fuel combustion is heat. The EU ETS has provided companies with the incentive to capture this waste heat and use it as a resource. Twence, a regional waste company in the Netherlands, captures the steam generated from its waste incineration and uses it to generate power. Furthermore, to reduce their CO_2 emissions and energy use, Twence and AkzoNobel, a salt company, teamed up in an innovative project involving steam. In their agreement, Twence transports its steam to the AkzoNobel salt factory via a pipeline. The steam is used by AkzoNobel in salt production to evaporate brine water and as a substitute for natural gas. AkzoNobel saves about 40 million cubic feet of natural gas every year and was able to cut its emissions by 72,000 tons of CO_2 per year as result of the project. This project was another direct result of the EU ETS.

Investing in GHG as an Asset Class

The EU ETS has given rise to several new kinds of investment opportunities in carbon. The most direct way is by taking a position in carbon allowances. This strategy can be accomplished via numerous carbon brokerage houses or exchanges that facilitate carbon trading. Fund managers and individual investors can respond to carbon risks and opportunities in a number of ways.

The first and most visible opportunity involves analyzing the carbon profiles of companies or investments and identifying the costs associated with their carbon footprints. Naturally, sectors that are more exposed to fossil-fuel combustion (such as utilities, oil and gas companies, and the cement sector) will be exposed to more carbon risk than the others. Similarly, the analyst may find geographical or regional variations in carbon exposure arising from regulatory and operational differences. A multinational company, in particular, has to manage a wide range of carbon regimes that are determined by the location of the multinational's operations. Carbon liabilities in portfolios can be managed by shifting positions from more carbon-intensive holdings to less carbon-intensive holdings within a sector. By doing so, the sectoral allocation remains unaltered. Investors can also follow a carbon-weighting approach to their portfolios and rebalance regularly to optimize their holdings from a carbon-exposure standpoint. A variety of index products exist that provide carbon-optimized exposure, including the S&P US Carbon Efficient Index, UBS Europe Carbon Optimized Index, DB Platinum CROCI Carbon Alpha TR Fund, and BNP Paribas EasyETF Low Carbon 100 Europe.

As discussed in the following subsections, investors can access carbon investments in numerous ways, ranging from the commodity markets to carbon project development funds.

Commodity Markets. The most direct way to get exposure to the asset class of carbon-related investments is by taking a position in spot, futures, or options markets for EUA allowances. The major exchanges trading EUA spot and futures contracts are, in this order, the IntercontinentalExchange (ICE), Chicago Mercantile Exchange, European Energy Exchange, and NASDAQ OMX. ICE, which has emerged as the primary marketplace for European emissions, has a market share of more than 90% of the exchange-traded fund (ETF) volume in the EUA futures market. An interesting note is that the EUA futures volume on ICE now surpasses that of Brent oil futures.

Equity Vehicles. Stock picking based on climate risk exposure can have an impact on the overall portfolio return as well as on risks. It is becoming increasingly important for investors to assess environmental performance as they would assess financial performance. Important factors include a company's EUA exposure, its emissions, its energy efficiency, its position on alternative energy, and available alternatives to reduce emissions. An analysis of the carbon risks in UK equity funds conducted by Trucost, an environmental cost accounting organization, found significant differences in carbon costs across individual equities, sectors, and regions.[73] Trucost analyzed 2,380 listed companies held in 118 equity portfolios and found overall exposure of 134 million tons of CO_2 equivalent (or CO_2e) and £1.6 billion to £7.6 billion in carbon potential allowance costs.[74] The carbon footprint of the aggregate portfolios was 582 tons of CO_2e per £1 million invested, on average, although significant variation was found among individual funds. Sectors with significant carbon risk included utilities, basic resources, construction, oil and natural gas, and food and beverages. Overall, the top four contributors to a portfolio's carbon footprint were RWE AG, International Power, American Electric Power, and BP.

---

[73]Trucost, "Carbon Risks in UK Equity Funds" (6 July 2009): www.trucost.com/_uploads/downloads/Carbon_Risks_in_UK_Equity_Funds.pdf. Accessed 4 October 2013.

[74]Carbon dioxide equivalency is a relationship that describes for a given mixture and amount of greenhouse gas, the amount of CO_2 that would have the same global warming potential when measured over a specified timescale (generally, 100 years). Please see Appendix B for the definitions and calculations of CO_2 equivalency.

Exchange-Traded Funds and Notes. ETFs and exchange-traded notes (ETNs) exist for retail investors interested in EUAs. Most of these instruments provide exposure by holding EUA futures contracts. Some of them are as follows:

- *iPath Global Carbon ETN (NYSE Arca: GRN).* This product, launched in June 2008, tracks the Barclays Capital Global Carbon Index Total Return.[75] The index currently includes two carbon-related credits: EUAs (88%) and CERs (12%).

- *ETFS Carbon ETC (LON: CARB and CARP).*[76] These products are designed to track the price of carbon emissions allowance futures. They track the ICE ECX EUA futures contract, which is traded in London on the ICE Futures Market. CARB and CARP are backed by matching fully funded swap contracts purchased from an entity of the Royal Dutch Shell Group. The product has been listed since October 2008 and trades in British pounds (CARP) or euros (CARB).

Clean Technology Companies. Picking companies that supply clean energy technologies allows investors to gain direct exposure to carbon as an asset class. In recent years, rapid increases in clean energy deployment have occurred in response to climate and renewable energy policies. In 2012, the clean energy sector recorded 88 gigawatts of additional generating capacity and $269 billion in investments. Investing in clean technology can take the form of investing in, specifically, solar, "smart grid," wind, biofuels, and similar companies.

Solar, in particular, has been drawing much attention because of the drop in panel-manufacturing costs combined with third-party financing and retail investments. With $126 billion invested, solar technologies attracted more investments than any other clean energy technology in 2012. Top names in the sector include Suntech Power (OTCBB: STP), which is the largest producer of silicon panels; First Solar (NASDAQ: FSLR), which produces low-cost thin-film solar panels; Sharp Solar (TYO: 6753); and Yingli Green Energy (NYSE: YGE). China, Europe, and the United States were the top markets for solar investments in 2012.

Wind energy has long been an important component of the clean energy mix. In 2012, the sector attracted about $73 billion in investments. Top wind-generation companies by market share are Dutch-based Vestas Wind Systems (CPH: VWS), China's Sinovel Wind (SHA: 601558) and Goldwind Global (HK: 2208), Spain's Gamesa (MCE: GAM), Germany's ENERCON

---

[75]The Barclays Carbon Index is discussed in Chapter 8.
[76]LON is the London Stock Exchange.

(private) and Siemens (NSE: SIEMENS), India-based Suzlon Energy (BOM: 532667), and General Electric Wind Energy (NYSE: GE) from the United States.[77]

Another exciting development is smart grid technology. A smart grid allows utilities and consumers to communicate with each other through intelligent technologies that result in better energy use and reliability. Several companies have jumped into development of this emerging technology and associated infrastructure. Major players include the Swiss company ABB (NYSE: ABB); Aclara Technologies (FRA: ET7), a smart grid facilitator that also develops advanced metering infrastructure; Alstom Grid (private), which provides equipment and services to the power sector; General Electric (NYSE: GE), which provides smart grid hardware and software services; and Siemens, whose smart grid portfolio includes switches and protection gear, substation automation, and wind and solar power products.

Companies involved in developing and building carbon capture and storage technologies form another class of investment opportunity. Most large companies that service the power sector are involved, including Halliburton (NYSE: HAL), KBR (NYSE: KBR), Shell (LON: RDSA), Fluor (NYSE: FLR), ABB (NYSE: ABB), and Mitsubishi Heavy Industries (TYO: 8058).

Companies that are involved in improving energy efficiency include Siemens, United Technologies (NYSE: UTX), Johnson Controls (NYSE: JCI), and ABB.

Related opportunities exist in the transportation space. Transportation, the second-largest source of emissions after power generation, has been shifting to cleaner forms of energy. Electric automotive companies (e.g., Tesla Motors [NASDAQ: TSLA]), natural gas transportation (e.g., Clean Energy Fuels [NASDAQ: CLNE]), and fuel efficient air transportation (e.g., European Aeronautic Defence and Space Company and Boeing [NYSE: BA]) are all worthy of attention. The EU ETS does not include transportation, so, given the focus of this chapter, we do not delve in great detail into these companies and technologies.

Climate Funds. Investors can also consider investments in the climate solutions field. This category includes the subcategories of energy efficiency, clean technologies, and renewable energy supplies. Examples of funds that invest specifically in companies that provide solutions are the following:

---

[77]CPH is the Copenhagen Stock Exchange, SHA is the Shanghai Stock Exchange, and BOM is the Bombay Stock Exchange.

- *Jupiter Climate Change Solutions (FSX: FGV7; ISIN: LU0300038618).*[78] An open-end fund incorporated in Luxembourg, Jupiter's objective is long-term capital growth from investment in companies worldwide. The fund invests in equities and equity-related securities of companies providing products or services that contribute to environmental improvement and facilitate adaptation to the impact of climate change. The fund is listed in Frankfurt.

- *F&C Global Climate Opportunities Fund (ISIN: LU0318451738).* This fund aims to achieve long-term capital appreciation by investing at least two-thirds of its total assets in equities and equity-related securities of companies that have substantial activities in alternative energy, energy efficiency, sustainable mobility, waste management, advanced materials, forestry and agriculture, water, acclimatization, and support services.

Listed Climate Companies. Another direct way to get carbon exposure is to take a position in listed initial public offerings (IPOs) of companies active in the carbon allowance space. Several companies issued listed IPOs at the height of the EUA market. They include companies that have an interest in generating and holding emission allowances or offsets—that is, project developers and funds—as well as companies engaged in ancillary services to the emissions-trading industry. (Commodity exchanges are among the ancillary services.)

Listed Carbon Project Development Funds. The broad class of funds in this category includes originators and developers of carbon allowance–generating projects and traders of carbon credits. The investment strategy in these funds involves deploying capital to either purchase carbon credits at reasonable prices or gain exposure to assets whose value is closely linked to the carbon credit price. This strategy includes (1) making investments through equity and debt instruments and (2) purchasing forward emissions contracts and interests in clean energy projects and companies. Investments in clean energy projects include ownership interests in waste-to-electricity projects, hydroelectric power, biodiesel manufacturing, carbon-trading brokerages, agricultural manure digesters, and wind power projects.

These funds manage a diverse set of assets with carbon exposure. Such assets include CERs, private equity investments, and cash and other assets. The portfolio companies seek to commercialize their carbon portfolios through derivatives markets and over-the-counter contracts.

---

[78]FSX is the Frankfurt Stock Exchange: www.boerse-frankfurt.de/en/funds/jupiter+climate+ change+solutions+fonds+LU0231118026.

In the past, several of these funds depended on carbon revenues to maintain a healthy balance sheet. The global carbon market, however, experienced major policy uncertainties that were triggered, in part, by lack of US action on climate change under Kyoto, the financial crisis, and the accompanying economic slowdown. These macro events caused severe losses for carbon portfolios during the 2008–13 period. Price declines in the carbon allowance market, for CER prices in particular, led to losses in many of these entities. In retrospect, investors would have benefited from shorting these funds.[79]

The core lesson for many of the listed carbon funds was that a high degree of correlation between the company's asset base and carbon prices presents a risk.

Listed Exchanges. Another environmental investment worthy of mention is the listed exchanges. Note that the exchanges' valuations are related to transaction volumes rather than transaction prices. When market volatility rose, the exchanges typically experienced greater transactions and more revenues. One such opportunity was Climate Exchange.[80]

Climate Exchange (CLE) owns spot and derivatives exchanges globally, on which major classes of environmental financial products are traded. The company began in 2004 as the Chicago Climate Exchange. Exchanges held by Climate Exchange include the Chicago Climate Exchange, Chicago Climate Futures Exchange, and European Climate Exchange as well as Environmental Derivatives Exchanges in Canada, Australia, and China. The exchanges held by CLE have the largest market share and most diverse set of financial products in the environmental finance sector. CLE was listed in the alternative investment market division of the London Stock Exchange (LSE). CLE also was the first exchange to list environmental derivatives contracts on North American domestic carbon programs, such as the Regional Greenhouse Gas Initiative and the California project (discussed later).

At its height, CLE was valued at more than $2.2 billion with a share price of a little more than £20 per share. The stock price declined in late 2009 because of uncertainty about US climate policy. Its European business had a market share of more than 90% in the EU ETS, however, with significant latent growth potential. In 2010, ICE bought CLE for $600 million, causing CLE's initial investors to experience a return of seven times the initial investment over an eight-year period. **Figure 4.6** is a graph of CLE's stock price from 2003 to 2010.

---

[79]Although many of these funds have not been financially successful, this observation should not be interpreted as a recommendation to either buy or sell them. The future performance of these funds cannot be inferred from past performance.

[80]Richard Sandor, one of the authors of this book, is a founder and chairman of Climate Exchange plc and its associated companies/subsidiaries.

Figure 4.6. CLE Stock Prices on the LSE, 2003–2010

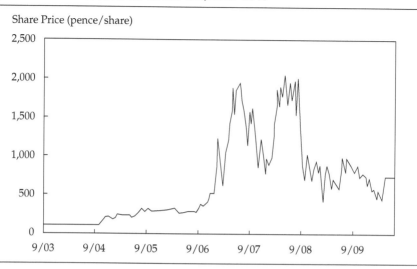

The CLE story is an example of the diverse opportunities that exist for gaining exposure to the carbon market without directly holding carbon allowances. Given the CLE experience, readers can see that listed financial exchanges are an interesting way to gain exposure to environmental assets. Seven exchanges cater to the EUA market. ICE, with more than 90% of the liquidity, is the predominant marketplace for EUAs. Others include the NASDAQ OMX and Chicago Mercantile Exchange (CME).

As emerging economies consider markets for carbon allowances or other environmental derivatives, such investments as CLE may emerge in those economies. In large growing economies—for example, India and China—that are introducing financial reforms and innovations into their derivatives industry in parallel with environmental policy considerations, new exchanges for trading of environmental derivatives may arise.[81] Already, exchanges in Tianjin in northern China and Shanghai exist exclusively for environmental allowance trading. The China Emissions Exchange in Shenzhen started trading carbon intensity in June 2013.[82] Other exchanges, such as the Multi Commodity Exchange of India and the National Stock Exchange of India, have experience with environmental contracts.

Other GHG Emissions–Trading Programs

The EU ETS is by far the largest GHG emissions–trading program, but other, smaller domestic and voluntary programs present some opportunities.

[81]For a detailed review, see Sandor, *Good Derivatives*, op cit.
[82]China Emissions Exchange: www.cerx.cn/cn/index.aspx. Accessed 4 October 2013.

This section describes some of these programs, beginning with those in the United States.

US Domestic Programs. The US opportunities are largely confined to emissions-trading programs in California and the northeastern United States. Although other regions are actively in the process of designing their own GHG reduction measures, these two regions are active and in play.

  ▓ *California's cap-and-trade program.* The California program has the potential to be one of the world's largest and most influential carbon-trading programs. The California economy is the 12th largest in the world, and it accounts for 13% of US gross domestic product, rivaling even some large national economies, such as that of India.[83] Therefore, the California program can have a significant impact on the global economy and environment. In addition, with its tendency to foster entrepreneurship, California has been the center of innovation in the United States for technology and, to some extent, for the agricultural and automotive sectors. Similar innovation is true for environmental finance. California was one of the early adopters of renewable energy and energy-efficiency policy. We discuss these policies in greater detail in Chapter 5.

The California emissions-trading program that began operating in January 2013 is currently the largest and most comprehensive emissions program in the United States. The program has its roots in the 2006 passage of the California Global Warming Solutions Act, AB 32 (i.e., Assembly Bill 32). AB 32 mandates that California's GHG emissions return to 1990 levels by 2020. The California Air Resources Board was charged with developing rules and regulations for implementing the program. The program covers 85% of the state's GHG emissions, includes all six GHGs, and trades through an emissions currency called the "California Carbon Allowance" (CCA).

The first compliance period is 2013–2014, in which stationary sources in industry and electrical power generation emitting 25,000 tons of CO_2e per year are covered, including electricity imports. The first commitment period seeks to achieve a reduction of 2% each year. The allowance budget for 2013 is about 162.8 million tons, which puts the market value of the allowances at $2.38 billion.

The second compliance period is 2015–2017, in which the targeted rate of emission reduction rises to 3% per year. In addition, the law now applies to distributors of fuel for transportation as well as residential and commercial use. The third compliance period is 2018–2020, with the targeted rate of reduction remaining at 3% per year.

---

[83]The GDP of California is $1.9 trillion and is greater than that of India (where the latter is not adjusted for purchasing power parity).

Several of the design mechanisms that were introduced earlier in the chapter are relevant here. First, California allows for a range of offset credits to be eligible for environmental compliance.[84] Compliance offset credits can be bought from projects anywhere in North America. Second, California allows banking of CCAs for future use but not borrowing of credits. Third, California allows for international offset linkage for projects in developing countries in selected sectors, such as tropical deforestation and forestry. The program is also open to the possibility of purchasing credits from other regulatory programs that may institute their own systems.

In contrast with the EU ETS, California's rules also incorporate price limits. In California, a price floor is set for the auction of the California allowances.[85]

There is a possibility of linking the California cap-and-trade program with other international emission systems. In April 2013, California announced plans to link its carbon program with the Canadian province of Quebec. Furthermore, California is in discussions to potentially link its program with China and Australia. These developments suggest that we may well see the rise of a global carbon market via the linking of regional systems rather than through national systems.

California allowances are traded as futures and options contracts on ICE and the CME. In addition, several environmental brokers broker these allowances.

Figure 4.7 presents historical volumes and open interest for California allowances from the ICE futures market, and **Figure 4.8** presents historical settlement prices. Interest in California allowances has been rising in light of the positive policy developments we have discussed. In the three months after the contract was listed on ICE, the open interest in California allowances had become greater than the Random Length Lumber futures contract listed on the Chicago Board of Trade for the same period and was rising quickly.[86]

▨ *Regional Greenhouse Gas Initiative.* Like California, the northeastern United States has been a center for innovation and fostering new markets. The region was among the first to launch mandates for renewable energy and energy efficiency. The region has been similarly active for carbon-related products: It launched the Regional Greenhouse Gas Initiative (RGGI) in 2009 as the first mandatory GHG emissions–trading scheme in the United States. RGGI covers emissions from power plants in the 10 northeastern and mid-Atlantic states through 2018. The first RGGI compliance period

---

[84]Up to 8% of CCAs may be accounted for by offsets, which fall into several categories.

[85]The price floor for California allowances was set at $10 per allowance in 2013, to increase annually by 5% over inflation.

[86]As of 22 July 2013, open interest in California Carbon Allowance futures and options on ICE was 27,403; that of Random Length Lumber futures and options was 6,990.

Figure 4.7. California Carbon Allowance Weekly Volume and Daily Open Interest, August 2011–September 2012

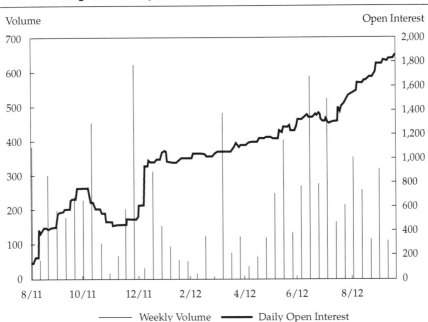

Notes: Measured at the ends of the months. Volume represents the total amount of trading activity or contracts that have changed hands in a given commodity market for a time period. Open Interest is the total number of outstanding contracts that are held by market participants at the end of each day.

Source: ICE.

was completed in 2011. The RGGI program included a price floor for its allowances.[87]

The program provides some valuable lessons for designers of other GHG programs. In the first compliance period, the actual emissions of the aggregate participating states were about 121 million metric tons of CO_2, although the allowance cap was set at 188 million metric tons. Because actual emissions were 36% lower than the cap, a severe oversupply of RGGI credits occurred. The reasons for the lower emissions include fuel switching, energy-efficiency measures, and weather. The overallocation problem led the allowance prices to reflect the annual price floor that was established for the first compliance period. RGGI prices hence tracked the price floors of $1.86 in 2010 and $1.89 in 2011.

---

[87]Regional Greenhouse Gas Initiative fact sheet: www.rggi.org/docs/RGGI_Auctions_in_Brief.pdf. Accessed 4 October 2013.

Figure 4.8. California Carbon Allowance Daily Settlement Price, August 2011–September 2012

Note: Measured at the ends of the months.

Source: ICE.

The second compliance period for RGGI runs from 2012 to 2014. New Jersey, however, announced its withdrawal from the program in the second phase, leaving only nine participants. The annual cap for this period has been set at 165 $MtCO_2e$, much above the current emissions trajectory. Further rule changes are under consideration at the time of writing this book.

Trading in RGGI allowances can be done through futures and options contracts listed on ICE and the CME. In addition, several emission brokers, including Evolution Markets, Amerex, and Tradition, broker in RGGI trades. **Figure 4.9** is a depiction of historical RGGI prices.

Voluntary Carbon Markets. In addition to the mandated regional programs just described, a market for GHG credits has been generated through projects approved under various voluntary programs. These credits are purchased mainly by corporations for their corporate social responsibility, carbon neutrality, and other green commitments. The most prominent of these programs is Verified Carbon Standard (VCS). A wide range of GHG offset projects globally source allowances to the VCS and trade through Verified Carbon Units. The price of these credits is determined by a wide range of factors, including project type, country, nature of GHG-reducing activity, and other social and environmental attributes, although the price can also be

Figure 4.9.   RGGI Price, August 2008–February 2012

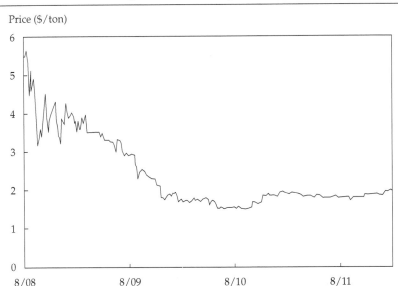

Note: Prices as of the 15th of the month.

Source: ICE emissions market data: www.theice.com/market_data.jhtml. Accessed 4 October 2013.

affected by the international CER price. These credits are mainly bought and sold through carbon brokers or intermediaries that purchase allowances from brokers and sell them to businesses and individuals.

The voluntary carbon market caters to an interesting class of offset projects that exist mainly outside or in advance of the UN CER system. These projects foster biodiversity and pursue such social goals as the empowerment of women and the alleviation of poverty. One such project category particularly worth describing involves carbon projects that seek to preserve tropical rain forests. A market called "Reducing Emissions from Deforestation and Degradation" (REDD) operates by generating REDD allowances that can be used as carbon offsets. By purchasing REDD credits, corporations not only prevent carbon loss from deforestation but also prevent deforestation itself and promote such environmental goals as biodiversity, waterway preservation, the protection of indigenous people and their habitats, and the conservation of a wide variety of other ecosystem assets. For example, mining companies that degrade tropical forests can purchase REDD credits to demonstrate their commitment to offset their environmental activities.

Such countries as Peru, Indonesia, Congo, and Brazil are leading the development of these projects. Peru is already a leader in the emerging environmental markets, as evidenced by the protection of its rich tropical forests.

REDD projects in Peru are in more advanced stages of development than those elsewhere. Peru currently hosts four REDD projects under the VCS, which, in the aggregate, have generated roughly 9 million carbon credits. Peru also has been ahead of others in terms of REDD readiness.

Conclusion

This chapter provided an overview of today's major programs to reduce GHG emissions. The market mechanisms and the nature of risk and opportunity, rather than the specifics of each program, should be the focus for the reader. This knowledge will assist in evaluating other emissions markets and products that emerge in the future.

The success of the EU ETS, in spite of the current debate about EUA prices, has led to emissions-trading programs getting off to promising starts around the world. This progress has taken place in the context of increased global efforts to tackle climate change. Australia announced a nationwide cap-and-trade scheme, expected to start in 2015, that will cover 60% of the country's annual GHG emissions. Mexico and South Korea have their own comprehensive climate bills, each passed in April 2012. India and China have set up markets that may be precursors to carbon trading. India is tackling its GHG emissions via a national renewable energy–trading program and a scheme for trading energy efficiency called "Perform, Achieve and Trade." Some cities around the world—Tokyo, for one—have prepared or are preparing their own schemes.

Perhaps the biggest opportunity will be the emerging carbon-trading program in China. As mentioned, China is the largest contributor to global GHG emissions and the second-largest economy in the world. China has advanced plans to pilot seven provincial emissions-trading schemes that could ultimately become the largest markets for carbon trading. A national scheme is expected to follow, although many of its features, including whether caps will be absolute or intensity based, remain unclear. Developments in China and California may ultimately shape the future of global emissions trading.[88]

The most recent goal of the UN Framework Convention on Climate Change, agreed to in Doha, Qatar, in 2012, is a limit on GHG emissions intended to be achieved by 2020 and designed to hold the cumulative total global temperature rise to 2° Celsius or less.[89]

---

[88]A map illustrating the emerging and existing emissions-trading schemes around the world is available online at https://icapcarbonaction.com/news-archive/153-icap-launches-interactive-emissions-trading-scheme-ets-map.

[89]The 2° Celsius limit has been determined as a critical threshold to prevent further negative impact from climate change.

These targets were set by international negotiations after careful consideration of the stage of economic growth of each mandated country. However, although about 90 countries have indicated plans for reducing emissions by 2020, the gap between current GHG emissions and the desired goal is widening. Even with the best efforts, global emissions by 2020 are expected to reach 49 billion tons (against an admissible level of 42 billion tons). Unless a variety of mitigation and adaptation strategies is used soon, the world will fall short of required emission reductions.

Therefore, the need for a broad range of management strategies across economies will create risks and opportunities and lead to GHG emissions reduction is urgent. Because of the increasingly evident effects of climate change, governments will be unable to ignore this need, even if progress is challenging. Confronting climate change will require technology, regulation, human resources, capacity building, and adaptation.

The emissions-trading model, when structured properly and deployed as an overall framework for climate mitigation, provides several opportunities for choice of efficient technological alternatives. The efficient market does not care what method for reducing GHGs is used and, therefore, selects a portfolio of mitigation avenues that optimizes the tradeoffs between attaining the emission-reduction goals and the cost of achieving them.

A wide variety of sectoral and regional policies has emerged to manage GHGs and other energy and environmental objectives. For example, in addition to reducing GHG emissions, renewable energy facilities have value in creating energy diversity and a cleaner electrical grid. The same is true for energy efficiency, reduction of deforestation, and a host of other socially desirable outcomes. The next chapter describes some of the related environmental markets that price these attributes.

5. Clean Energy Markets and Associated Asset Classes

The primary policy response to global warming around the world has been the implementation of market-based programs for the reduction of greenhouse gas emissions. Several additional markets and practices, however, have had an impact on climate change and the broader environment. These markets include renewable energy certificates (RECs), renewable identification numbers (RINs), and crediting for energy efficiency. RECs represent the property rights to the environmental, social, and other nonpower qualities of renewable electricity generation.[90] RINs play a role somewhat similar to that of RECs but in the market for transportation fuels. Both markets are in their infancy in terms of trading, but they have the potential to reach reasonable volumes because the underlying values for both are in excess of $1 billion.

Although no traded market for energy efficiency truly exists (except in a few states that have included it as part of RECs or alternative energy standards), it represents one of the largest opportunities to save money on energy expenditures and reduce emissions. It is also important because energy efficiency, even when not directly credited, affects the prices of other markets, including CO_2 and RINs.

RECs developed as an outgrowth of consumer demand for renewable sources of electricity in the late 1990s and requirements that several states put in place to meet targets for renewable energy generation, called "renewable portfolio standards" (RPS). RECs allowed investors to purchase the environmental attributes of renewable energy without having to purchase the actual power. This decoupling made it possible for RECs to, in effect, become a new type of currency for renewable energy projects. One revenue stream could be realized from the sale of the power, and another, from the sale of the RECs. Much like the GHG markets, RECs trade in both voluntary and mandatory markets.

RINs were developed in large part in response to the desire of midwestern states in the United States to help foster growth in agriculture-based renewable transportation fuels. RINs are a product of the US Renewable Fuel Standard (RFS), which requires transportation fuel that is produced and consumed in the United States to contain a percentage of renewable fuels. RINs are effectively a tracking mechanism for the RFS that allows the US EPA to determine whether a company is in compliance with the mandate.

---

[90]Renewable Energy Certificates, US Environmental Protection Agency: www.epa.gov/greenpower/gpmarket/rec.htm.

Of all the mechanisms addressing climate change and the broader impacts of energy production on the environment, none is probably more significant than energy efficiency. The International Energy Agency estimates that implementing energy-efficiency measures in buildings, industrial processes, and transportation could cut global demand by one-third by 2050.

In this chapter, we first describe the REC and RIN markets—in particular, the policy changes that brought these markets into being, general market characteristics, how RECs and RINs are traded and tracked, and opportunities for investors in the REC and RIN markets. Second, we discuss the importance of energy efficiency.

Renewable Energy Certificates

Currently, in the United States, 29 states plus the District of Columbia and Puerto Rico have state-level renewable portfolio standards.[91] Many large states, including California, Texas, New York, and Illinois, have these standards. Most states use the US Department of Energy (DOE) definition of "renewable," which consists of the following categories of energy generation: wind, concentrated solar thermal, distributed and centralized photovoltaic, biomass, hydro, geothermal, landfill gas, and ocean power. Typically, however, some specialized requirements exist in various state RPS. For example, the state of New Jersey requires that 20.38% of electricity come from renewables by 2020–2021, with an additional requirement that 4.1% of electricity come from solar sources by 2027–2028.[92]

RECs reflect the "green" attributes of electricity that is generated from renewable energy sources. These certificates are important because they can be a motivating factor for building renewable energy facilities. RECs allow these green attributes to be sold or bought separately from the physical electricity generated from renewable sources. Thus, an owner of a wind farm can have two sources of revenue: from selling electricity and from selling RECs. One REC represents the attributes that are associated with 1 megawatt hour (MWh) of energy from a renewable source. RECs are often assigned a "vintage," usually the year in which the renewable energy is generated.

Renewable Energy Legislation in the United States. The idea of unbundling the attributes of renewable energy from the underlying electricity was first discussed in a design document for the California RPS in

---

[91]Map of Portfolio Standard Policies, Database of State Incentives for Renewables and Efficiency, North Carolina Solar Center (March 2013): www.dsireusa.org/documents/summarymaps/RPS_map.pdf.
[92]New Jersey Incentives/Policies for Renewables & Efficiency, Database of State Incentives for Renewables and Efficiency, North Carolina Solar Center: www.dsireusa.org/incentives/incentive.cfm?Incentive_Code=NJ05R.

1995–1996.[93] A number of proposals, such as renewable energy credit trading, were made to the California Public Utilities Commission, but the idea was not adopted.

The same idea came up in 1997 during discussions about implementing environmental disclosure on electricity labels in New England. Stakeholders were concerned with the validity of the fuel mix and emissions level claims of the electricity providers. A potential solution was to separate the electricity itself from various attributes of its generation.

In 1998, electricity markets in California, Massachusetts, and Rhode Island were opened up to retail choice. Automated Power Exchange (APX), which was eventually designated as the regional REC-tracking authority, opened a separate market for green power the day before the California market officially commenced on 1 April 1998. This market was a wholesale market for scheduled electricity deliveries; it was designed to help electricity providers differentiate themselves and their products. The APX Green Power Market traded electricity generated by renewable resource technologies as defined by the California legislation and under its renewable energy programs. One month later, in May 1998, the first retail REC product (called the "Regen") was sold in Massachusetts.[94] One year later, APX began a market for "green tickets." These wholesale products were purchased and "rebundled" with commodity electricity for retail green power sales.

In June 1999, Texas adopted Senate Bill 7, a restructuring law that included a renewable portfolio standard. The law also resulted in the first renewable energy credit–trading program in the United States. That December, the Public Utility Commission of Texas adopted the rules required for a credit-trading program.[95]

The United States is crisscrossed by various REC tracking systems. These tracking systems closely (although not exactly) mirror the electricity grid of the United States. The lack of a national electric grid creates a variety of complications, not only for delivering power between regions of the grid but also for renewables. Because of the fragmented nature of the grid, exporting renewable power into some states with aggressive renewable energy mandates, such as California, is sometimes difficult. This factor can complicate the development of renewables in states where renewable resources are plentiful (i.e., solar power in Arizona or wind power in South Dakota) because transmission access to states with large demands for renewable power is constrained.

---

[93]Much of the information in this section is from the US EPA Green Power Partnership's website on renewable energy certificates: www.epa.gov/greenpower/gpmarket/rec.htm.

[94]Retail RECs are those sold to individuals or small businesses.

[95]A map of these systems may be found at www.epa.gov/greenpower/gpmarket/tracking.htm.

Types of REC Programs. REC markets usually fall into two broad categories: *compliance* RECs that are used to meet state RPS requirements and *voluntary* RECs that consumers and companies buy/sell to match their electricity needs on a voluntary basis. In both markets, RECs can be sold separately or bundled with the sale of commodity electricity. More than 50 actively traded compliance REC markets are in operation; several states have multiple REC markets. The most actively traded markets are PJM Interconnection (New Jersey, in particular), New England Power Pool (NEPOOL) in Connecticut and Massachusetts, and the Electric Reliability Council of Texas.

■ *Compliance market.* In 2011, 31 separate RPS markets were in operation.[96] RPS policies collectively required utilities to obtain 133 million MWh from renewable energy sources, roughly 3% of the total megawatt hours produced in the United States.[97] As with the cap-and-trade markets for GHGs and sulfur dioxide, if electric utilities do not meet the mandated levels of renewable energy production, they can purchase RECs in the market. Similarly, if they produce more renewable energy than their mandates, they can sell their excess RECs in the market.

In compliance markets, REC transfers are performed through such tracking systems as NEPOOL, the PJM Generation Attribute Tracking System, Texas Geographic Information Systems, Western Renewable Energy Generation Information System, and North American Renewables Registry. Currently, the REC compliance markets are most active in Texas, Connecticut, Massachusetts, and Maine.

The multiplicity of rules governing the eligibility of RECs is one of the main reasons the compliance REC market is so fragmented. REC markets are fragmented both within and between states. For example, a wind farm in Illinois may be able to sell RECs in Pennsylvania but the reverse may not be allowed. That same Illinois wind farm may not be able to sell RECs in Ohio, even though Ohio might accept RECs from a wind farm in Pennsylvania.[98] Additionally, state-level rules for specific types of renewables mean that a solar REC in New Jersey may not be fungible with a wind REC from New Jersey.

REC market eligibility depends on the resources available, state of origin, and commercial operation date of the renewable energy source. Other considerations may include specific fuel requirements, vintage, and energy-delivery

---

[96]A map of state-level RPS may be found at www.epa.gov/greenpower/gpmarket/tracking.htm.
[97]Platts, "Renewable Energy Certificates" (April 2012): www.platts.com/IM.Platts.Content/InsightAnalysis/IndustrySolutionPapers/RECSpecialReport1112.pdf.
[98]Peter Toomey, "REC Markets and Trading 101," 2011 WSPP Spring Operating Committee Meeting, Iberdrola Renewables (21 March 2011): www.wspp.org/filestorage/rec_markets_trading_wspp_oc_mtg_032211.pdf.

rules. To promote specific forms of renewable energy, some states adopt "multipliers" and "carve-outs." In multipliers, certain technologies receive more than 1 REC for 1 MWh of energy generated. The result is a financial incentive for energy companies to invest in the form of renewable energy that the state is using the multiplier to promote. But states can also use multipliers as a form of protectionism against out-of-state renewable energy generators, which severely limits interstate REC trading. Similarly, many state programs establish subtargets—carve-outs or "set-asides"—to promote certain renewable projects. For these subtargets, in addition to meeting the RPS mandates, energy companies need to prove that they have acquired a specific percentage of their power sales from the technology type required by the state in question. An example of this practice is solar RECs (SRECs). In some cases, multiple technology types are bundled together in "tiers" or "classes."

The complexity of rules governing RECs leads to a number of liquidity issues. Consider the previous case, in which RPS rules in two states were not reciprocal, which is usually the case. The RECs originating from Illinois wind farms are eligible under Pennsylvania's RPS, but Pennsylvania's wind-based RECs are not recognized under Illinois's RPS. Moreover, eligibility rules are often complex and ambiguous and are constantly changing to reflect state demands, a circumstance that can cause abrupt changes in the REC market. So, obviously RECs are not a homogeneous commodity and are subject to the whims of electorates and legislatures.

■ *Voluntary market.* The voluntary market for RECs is driven primarily by consumer demand for renewable electricity and corporate commitments to procure green energy. RECs are bought and sold as delivered renewable energy products (bundled with electricity) or bought and sold separately. The bundled product involves a wholesale transaction, whereas separate sales generally entail both wholesale and retail transactions.

The voluntary market is composed of utilities (more than 850 of them, according to the National Renewable Energy Laboratory, or NREL) that offer green power options to their customers, competitive electricity suppliers operating in states with retail competition, and marketers who sell RECs wholesale or retail. In 2009, the NREL estimated that 1.4 million US electricity customers voluntarily bought green power through utilities or competitive suppliers or voluntarily bought RECs from REC marketers. Although exact figures are not available, the NREL estimates that approximately 40 million MWh of voluntary RECs were purchased in 2011. The most active voluntary REC markets in terms of total green power sales can be found in California, Illinois, Maryland, Oregon, Texas, and Washington. **Table 5.1** summarizes the main differences between the voluntary and compliance REC markets.

Table 5.1. Summary of Differences between Compliance and Voluntary REC Markets

Criterion	Compliance Market	Voluntary Market
Demand driver	RPS, which mandates electricity Providers obtain a certain fraction of their electricity from renewable energy sources	Voluntary consumer demand, environmental disclosure, corporate commitments, carbon claims, and so on
Procurements	Bundled green power (power + RECs)	Bundled green power (power + RECs)
	Unbundled RECs alone	Unbundled RECs alone
Transaction types	Wholesale	Wholesale and retail
Market division	Regional markets (tracking system)	Utility green pricing programs and competitive green power market
	National markets	Voluntary unbundled REC market
Important price factor	Geographical region	Generation type
	Generation type (for specific standard)	Vintage
Price	Higher	Lower
Size of market	133 million MWh	40 million MWh

Table 5.2 provides a summary of the size, pricing, and notional value of four of the most actively traded REC markets in the United States. The full notional value of the REC market is difficult to determine because it is largely a brokered market in which prices and volumes traded are not consistently reported. Although the individual states' market shares are not large, the mandatory market is much larger than the voluntary market in megawatt hour terms.

Market Players in RECs. Compliance RECs are generally bought and sold by utilities and independent power producers to adhere to state mandates for renewable power production. Financial players are also involved in the compliance REC market, both as speculators and as owners of generating assets of renewable and nonrenewable power.

In the voluntary market, corporate buyers make up the bulk of REC purchases, often as part of their corporate sustainability efforts. Many of the largest purchasers are some of America's most recognizable corporate brands—for example, Intel, Microsoft, Walmart, Starbucks, and Whole Foods.[99] Individual households and small businesses can also purchase voluntary RECs, often through their local utilities.

In both the compliance and voluntary markets, RECs can be directly traded from buyer to seller via exchanges or through third-party marketers,

---

[99]A full list of the top buyers can be found on the EPA Green Power Partnership site: www.epa.gov/greenpower/toplists/top50.htm.

©2014 The CFA Institute Research Foundation

Table 5.2. Examples of State REC Markets

State	2010 Size (million MWh)	2010 Pricing ($/MWh)	2010 Notional Value (millions)	2020 Estimate Size (million MWh)	2020 Estimate Pricing ($/MWh)	2020 Estimate Notional Value (millions)
New Jersey: Class 1	5–10	8–15	$40–$120	15–20	8–15	$120–$300
Connecticut: Class 1	4–5	20–30	80–150	8–10	20–30	160–300
Massachusetts: Class 1	3–5	20–30	60–150	8–10	20–30	160–300
California: Tradable RECs	5–15	20–30	100–440	15–25	20–30	300–750

brokers, and asset managers. Many REC market participants are active in both the compliance and voluntary markets. REC marketers typically purchase RECs from renewable energy sources and resell them to utilities or end-users. REC brokers generally do not take ownership of the RECs at any point. Instead, they match sellers with buyers and make a profit on the commission. According to the DOE, 92 commercial and/or wholesale REC marketers, 25 retail marketers, 24 certificate brokers/exchanges, and 19 consumer protection/tracking systems are currently active. Additionally, four exchanges in the United States list REC products: the IntercontinentalExchange (ICE), Flett Exchange, Leaf Exchange, and Environmental Certificate Exchange.[100] ICE is currently the only regulated futures and options exchange offering REC contracts in the United States.

REC Pricing. Factors that affect REC prices in the individual state markets are usually the supply-and-demand dynamic created by the state mandate, generation technology, vintage, volume purchased, generation region, eligibility, and whether the RECs are bought to meet compliance obligations or to serve voluntary retail consumers. Natural gas prices and other forms of conventional generation can affect the cost competitiveness of renewable energy generation, which is reflected in REC prices. To the extent that emission reductions are an attribute of RECs, carbon credit prices may also affect REC prices.

The fragmentation and lack of homogeneity are compounded by opaqueness. REC prices are difficult to obtain except from a broker because most transactions are over-the-counter. Some pricing trends for REC classes can be found in sample data from brokers, such as ICAP and Evolution Markets, as well as in periodic disclosures in utility commission proceedings. Using data from these sources, we observed that prices for voluntary RECs are generally much lower than those for compliance RECs. As a result of the multiplicity of REC products, however, no centralized price reporting is publicly accessible, with the exception of products traded on ICE.[101]

■ *Compliance market.* State RPS requirements are the chief price determinants in compliance REC markets. The prices for compliance RECs can differ considerably by state and are also affected by resource quality (e.g., wind speed) and regional electricity prices. Currently, more than half of the state-level RPS programs are under threat of being pared back. This phenomenon has increased in recent years as declining natural gas prices have made renewable energy prices comparatively more expensive. Other price determinants include fungibility of RECs between states and the cost of specific renewable energy technologies.

---

[100]REC Marketers, the Green Power Network, US DOE: http://apps3.eere.energy.gov/greenpower/markets/certificates.shtml?page=2.

[101]*Climate Change Business Journal*, vol. 4, no. 6/7 (2011): www.3degreesinc.com/sites/default/files/CCBJ_Reprint3DegreesProfile.pdf.

As illustrated in **Figure 5.1**, REC prices for Massachusetts, New Jersey, and Connecticut have traded from highs of $50/MWh and $60/MWh to lows of less than $10/MWh. These northeastern states have relatively stringent RPS goals when compared with such states as Pennsylvania and Texas, where RECs consistently trade under $10/MWh. Meanwhile, REC prices remain under $5/MWh in Washington, DC, Delaware, Illinois, Maryland, New Jersey, Ohio, Pennsylvania, and Texas.

State-level carve-outs for specific types of renewable energy can also be a major driver in determining price. For example, SRECs are often priced 6–10 times above RECs generated by wind, biomass, and hydro sources. In fact, SREC prices hovered below $200/MWh in 2011, but for such states as Massachusetts and Ohio, prices have been as high as $400–$550/MWh and, occasionally, higher. SREC price information is disseminated via two online auction platforms—SRECTrade and Flett Exchange.

One state that presents a case study of not only carve-outs but also the impact of price signals on behavior is New Jersey. With one of the most aggressive RPS in the country, New Jersey has become a leading market in the United States for renewable energy—solar energy, in particular. New Jersey law requires a minimum of 20.38% of its sold electricity to come from renewables by the year 2021. It has an additional mandate that solar power contribute 4.1% of the power sold by 2028. The solar carve-out, established in 2006, has since been revised upward twice, most recently in 2012. Each of these policy interventions caused fairly dramatic responses in the market, which can be seen in **Figure 5.2**; the increased RPS requirement passed in 2012 caused an increase in prices as well as megawatts installed.

Figure 5.1. Historical OTC Price Ranges in Selected REC Markets

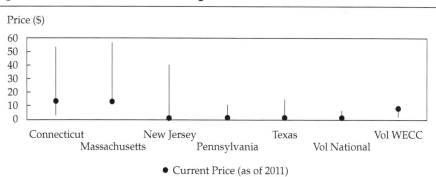

Notes: Prices are indicative and derived from broker information and simplified methodology. Near-term vintages only. Vol is volatility. National refers to the national REC market. WECC is the Western Electricity Coordinating Council.

Source: Toomey, "REC Markets and Trading 101," op cit.

Figure 5.2. Megawatts of Solar Installed in New Jersey by Month, 2009–2013, and Flett Exchange's NJ 2012 SREC Pricing, 2011–2013
(as of March 2013)

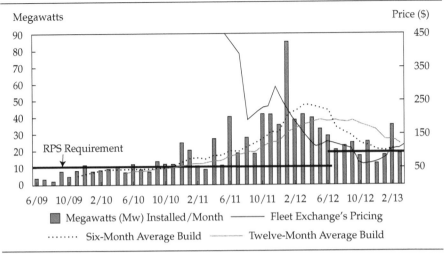

Note: March 2013 = 18 Mw; total = 1,026 Mw.

Source: Flett Exchange.

The market response to the solar carve-out in New Jersey illustrates several lessons that can be learned from our study of other environmental markets, such as those for SO2 and GHGs. In each case, the market responded to the price signal far more aggressively than most analysts expected, resulting in far greater subsequent price declines than many expected. Much like the installation of scrubbers for SO2 or the increase in fuel switching and energy efficiency in GHG markets, the New Jersey SREC market experienced price declines from a high of roughly $700 to less than $100 in less than two years.

Solar developers responded to the SREC incentive by plowing resources into the state, making it the third-highest generator of solar electricity, behind only California and Arizona, despite its relatively low amount of solar radiation. This price signal attracted the interest of not only utilities but also financial players, who entered the market as independent power producers by financing solar installations.

■ *Voluntary market.* Compliance RECs generally must be from sources in a certain region to comply with the RPS in that region. Voluntary RECs are free from geographical constraints, however, and can be sourced nationally. Nevertheless, with some exceptions, most utility green pricing programs and marketers source their RECs from local or regional resources. Nationally sourced voluntary RECs are often demanded by large corporations with facilities in multiple locations nationwide. For voluntary RECs, a premium can be gained if they are competing with compliance RECs or if they come from regions with limited renewable energy resources.

The prices of wholesale RECs used in the voluntary market are considerably different from those in the compliance market. Voluntary REC prices have generally traded in the range of $1/MWh to $10/MWh. The factors that determine the wholesale price differences are also not the same—that is, state-level RPS regulation is not a price driver because there is generally no fungibility between the voluntary and mandatory REC markets. In the voluntary market, more importance is given to the type and location of the renewable resource, the vintage, the volume purchased, and the level of competition created by compliance markets.

For example, **Figure 5.3** illustrates the price of western US wind RECs as compared with the price of nationally sourced wind RECS and any other nationwide renewable energy technology. As can be seen, from 2008 to 2012, western wind RECs fetched a premium over the nationally sourced wind RECs. The primary reason for this discrepancy is a strong supply of nationally sourced wind, which brings its REC price down.

Voluntary market retail prices for RECs tend to be higher than wholesale prices to allow marketers to recoup their costs and retain a profit. Because the

Figure 5.3. Voluntary REC Prices, January 2008–June 2012

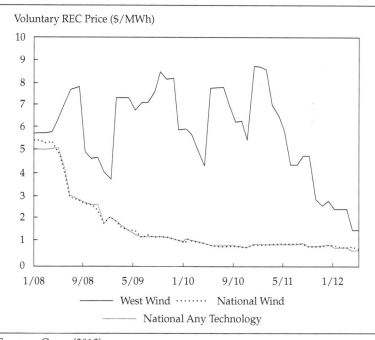

Source: Spectron Group (2012).

pricing of retail RECs is less heavily influenced by the location and vintage of the resource, however, the pricing shows more consistency among the states. But price does vary by the type and quality of the renewable resources used to supply the product.

In 2011, the retail sales of renewable energy in voluntary markets exceeded 35 million MWh, which is an 11% increase from 2010. Wind energy continues to dominate the newly built generation capacity in the US renewable energy market and, as a result, dominates the voluntary REC market also. As shown in the breakdown in **Figure 5.4**, in 2010, wind constituted 83.1% of total green power sales. Although the other categories of REC sales are quite small, some are very important in specific sectors or states in terms of providing an incentive for building new renewable power. The market for SRECs, for example, is still in its infancy in most states. SREC trading is expected to increase from more than 520 Mw in 2011 to nearly 7,300 Mw in 2025.

Investment Opportunities in RECs and Renewable Energy. Investors can purchase RECs directly by accessing one of the regulated or unregulated exchanges or brokers mentioned in the preceding sections. Depending on the type of REC and location, it will be registered at one of the REC registries. Alternatively, investors can invest in companies that generate RECs through the sale of renewable electricity or via the sale of products, such as wind turbines or solar panels. Other, but more limited, opportunities may exist to invest in RECs by taking an ownership stake in exchanges, brokerage firms, and REC registry and tracking companies. Additional and more indirect investment angles may take into account the effects that renewables have on

Figure 5.4.   Voluntary Market REC Sales Composition

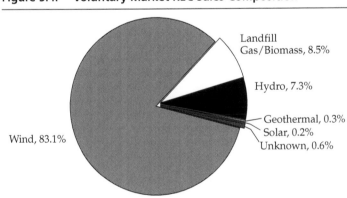

Source: Jenny Heeter and Lori Bird, "Status and Trends in U.S. Compliance and Voluntary Renewable Energy Certificate Markets (2010 Data)," National Renewable Energy Laboratory (October 2011): http://apps3.eere.energy.gov/greenpower/pdfs/52925.pdf.

other natural resources. For example, unlike fossil fuels, most renewables use little or no water, so investors may be able to combine investments in renewables with investments in water, which is discussed in the next chapter.

Wind turbine manufacturers—such as Suzlon Energy, Sinovel Wind Group, and Vestas Wind Systems—are companies with market capitalizations in the multibillion-dollar range that operate globally and trade on stock exchanges in Europe, China, and elsewhere. Their exposure to REC markets can be limited, particularly because wind energy has become increasingly less reliant on various subsidies to be competitive with traditional fossil fuel–based generation. Solar companies, although a tiny market overall, are still reliant on forms of subsidies, such as SRECs, to remain competitive. As the price of solar panels has dropped markedly in recent years, however, solar has become less reliant on subsidies than in the past and, in some cases, has become competitive with fossil-fuel generation, particularly in countries with demand for off-grid power supply. Companies that operate globally and are considered to be leaders in the field are First Solar, SunPower (NASDAQ: SPWR), and Yingli Green Energy.

Although exchange-traded funds provide little exposure to RECs, a wide variety of ETFs provide exposure to renewable energy. One of the first such ETFs was PowerShares WilderHill Clean Energy (NYSE: PBW). This ETF is based on the WilderHill Clean Energy Index, which lists green energy technology companies and some conventional energy companies. Top holdings as of 2012 were Amyris, Solazyme, and EnerNOC. Assets under management were approximately $133 million.

The Guggenheim Solar ETF (NYSE: TAN) follows the Claymore/ MAC Global Solar Energy Index. It includes not only panel manufacturers but also companies that specialize in other links in the solar value chain, such as solar consulting, marketing, and financing firms. Top holdings as of 2012 were GCL-Poly Energy Holdings, First Solar, and GT Advanced Technologies. Assets under management were approximately $71 million.

For wind exposure, several ETFs are available, including First Trust ISE Global Wind Energy Index Fund (NYSE: FAN). The fund's major holdings as of 2012 were EDP Renováveis, Iberdrola, China Longyuan Power Group, and Vestas Wind Systems. Assets under management were approximately $21 million.

Conclusion. Renewable energy provides environmental benefits beyond simply the electricity it generates. Cleaner air and water, healthier communities, and reduced GHG emissions are all by-products of renewable energy that are not usually priced into the energy itself. Renewable energy certificates provide a way to motivate the use of renewable energy where markets for these beneficial by-products do not readily exist. State and federal renewable energy mandates, together with voluntary RECs, are major drivers in the development of renewable energy in the United States.

REC programs exist in both voluntary and mandatory settings. Some programs emphasize wind generation; others focus on solar or geothermal power. In many cases, RECs can be the difference between a project being built and being shelved. Remember that the energy can be separated from the renewable attributes. Thus, RECs can be bought and sold separately from the power itself, and RECs are often sold in physical locations other than where the power is generated. This aspect provides an opportunity to trade RECs on a regional or even, in some instances, national basis.

Unfortunately, the REC markets are heterogeneous, opaque, illiquid, and fragmented. Because renewable portfolio standards are state-level policies, understanding RECs requires understanding many individual state-based markets. The lack of a national grid system and a national renewable portfolio standard compounds these problems of fragmentation. Thus, a potential investor in RECs must keep abreast of state-level political dynamics that may affect the market.

Renewable Identification Numbers

With the passage of the Energy Policy Act of 2005, the US Congress made the promotion of biofuels a priority. Biofuels are fuels generated from plant matter. The most common type in the United States is ethanol derived from corn.

The centerpiece of the Energy Policy Act is the Renewable Fuel Standard, which began under the 2005 act and was extended by the Energy Independence and Security Act of 2007. The RFS requires transportation fuel produced and consumed in the United States to contain a percentage of renewable fuel—typically, biofuel. The 2012 requirement for the RFS mandates that 15.2 billion gallons of renewable fuel be used. This percentage amounts to slightly more than 9% of the total volume of gasoline and diesel consumed in the United States in 2012.[102] The current RFS is set to run through 2022. The yearly mandates by fuel type are provided in **Figure 5.5**.

To track compliance with the RFS mandates, the EPA created a renewable identification number system. An RIN is a 38-digit number that is assigned to each gallon of renewable fuel produced in or imported into the United States. The numbers are used primarily by fuel refiners for compliance with their RFS requirements. Understanding RINs is important because biofuel use has broad implications for food and fuel prices and because investors

---

[102]EPA, "EPA Finalizes 2012 Renewable Fuel Standards," EPA Office of Transportation and Air Quality (December 2011): www.epa.gov/otaq/fuels/renewablefuels/documents/420f11044.pdf.

Figure 5.5. RFS Mandates by Type, 2008–2022

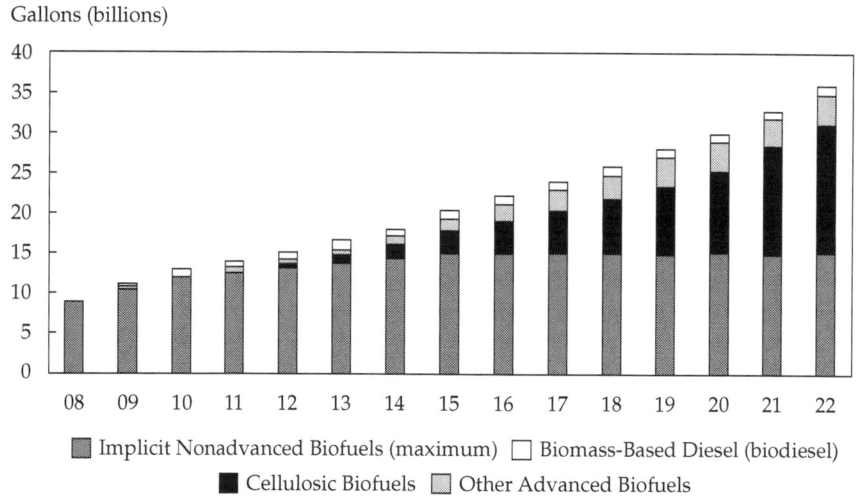

Gallons (billions)

Note: Calendar years.

Source: Lihong McPhail, Paul Westcott, and Heather Lutman, "The Renewable Identification Number System and U.S. Biofuel Mandates," US Department of Agriculture Economic Research Service, Outlook No. BIO-03 (November 2011).

may also speculate directly in RINs. Approximately 15 billion RINs were issued last year, and that number will only get larger over time. Their prices generally range from a couple of pennies to a couple of dollars; even at low prices, the underlying value can be significant because of the large quantity issued annually.

Once the traditional fossil fuel—typically, gasoline or diesel—is blended with the renewable fuel—typically, ethanol—the RIN can be separated from the fuel. Thus, an RIN can be traded. So, refiners, rather than blending the renewable fuel themselves, can purchase RINs from another refiner or blender if they find this option economically optimal. Alternatively, RINs can remain with the renewable fuel and be used for compliance by the "obligated party" (as defined under the law) or be held for future compliance. RINs are tracked by the EPA through its Moderated Transaction System. Access to the market is quite simple. Users must register with the EPA and establish an account with the EPA's Central Data Exchange. Transactions are then submitted electronically to the EPA.

Although most RINs are generated from ethanol blending, other types of renewable fuels are also eligible. Cellulosic ethanol and "advanced" biofuels (those not derived from corn) are encouraged under the RFS and have been mandated at increasingly higher levels over time. For instance, compressed or liquefied natural gas for vehicles—despite not being a renewable fuel—can also benefit from the RFS by receiving RINs for avoiding emissions from gasoline- and diesel-fueled vehicles, which generate more pollution than vehicles fueled by compressed or liquefied natural gas. These incentives provide a boost to alternative fuel manufacturers.

Compliance with the RFS mandates is assessed annually. If a refiner or other obligated party does not have a sufficient number of RINs to satisfy its individual mandate, it may carry that deficit into the following year, provided that the previous year's deficit is covered and the next year's obligation is met. If an obligated party has excess RINs, it may sell or bank them into the next year for compliance, provided that no more than 20% of the obligated party's current year's obligation is satisfied with banked RINs. RINs that go unused after a period of two years are retired.

In effect, obligated parties must meet four biofuel compliance targets, or renewable volume obligations. They are

- total renewable fuel,

- advanced biofuel,

- biomass-based diesel, and

- cellulosic biofuel.

Each gallon of fuel is weighted on the basis of its energy content relative to the energy content of ethanol and then adjusted for renewable content. In this formula, a gallon of traditional ethanol receives 1 RIN whereas a gallon of biodiesel receives 1.5 RINs, and so on.

The largest players in the RIN market are generally the largest refiners. Thus, Exxon Mobil (NYSE: XOM), BP (NYSE: BP), Chevron (NYSE: CVX), Marathon (NYSE: MRO), Sunoco (NYSE: SUN), and Valero Energy Corporation (NYSE: VLO) make up the list of the largest obligated parties under the RFS. Other important players are the ethanol companies. Although they do not receive RINs from producing ethanol, RINs have an impact on the value of their products. The largest US ethanol companies are Archer Daniels Midland (NYSE: ADM), POET (privately held), Valero, and Green Plains Renewable Energy (NASDAQ: GPRE).

RIN Pricing. RIN pricing is affected by a number of market and policy signals. Among the policy signals outside the RFS itself, which mandates the yearly level of ethanol and biofuel use, are ethanol blender tax credits, import tariffs, and crop subsidies. The Volumetric Ethanol Excise Tax Credit (VEETC) has perhaps the biggest policy-driven impact on RIN prices. The VEETC is available to ethanol blenders in the amount of $0.45 per gallon of ethanol blended with gasoline. The VEETC was introduced in 2004 and, because of its costs to the US taxpayer, which amounted to $21 billion in 2010, was frequently criticized and allowed to expire at the end of 2011. As a result, many analysts expected RIN prices to increase, which they did.

Among the market factors influencing RIN pricing are corn prices, crude oil prices, soybean prices, natural gas prices, and the prices of other commodities in the agricultural and energy spaces. For example, high corn prices can lead to decreased ethanol production and thus higher RIN prices. Conversely, high oil prices make substitute fuels like ethanol and biofuels more attractive, resulting in increased production and decreased values for RINs. In contrast, natural gas is a primary processing fuel for the ethanol industry. So, increases in the cost of natural gas result in increased production costs for ethanol, decreases in ethanol production, and increased values for RINs. Finally, fuel efficiency standards can have an indirect impact on RINs. As vehicles become more efficient, demand for fuel decreases, thus lowering the demand for RINs.

RINs are traded primarily OTC but are also listed on both the Chicago Mercantile Exchange and ICE. Because RINs are traded primarily OTC, no centralized source for price information on RINs is publicly available. Several private companies, such as Platts, Argus Media, and Oil Price Information Service, provide price histories for subscribers.

Figure 5.6.   Price of RINs in the Secondary Market, 4 April 2008–7 March 2013

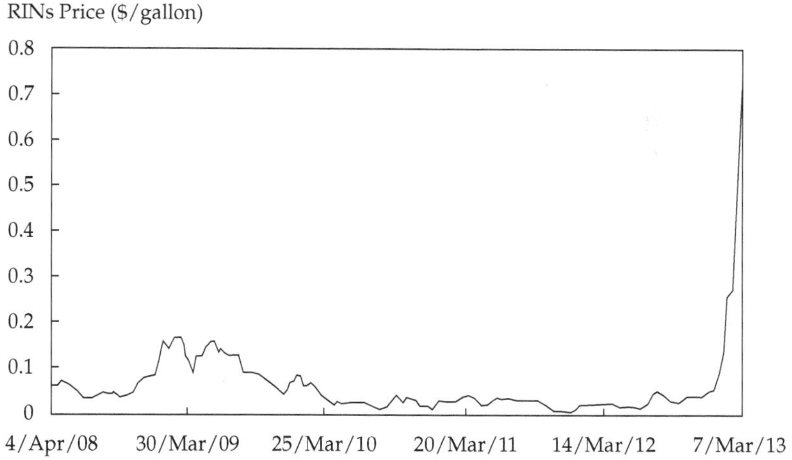

RINs Price ($/gallon)

Source: Scott Irwin and Darrel Good, "Exploding Ethanol RINs Prices: What's the Story?" *Farmdoc Daily*, Department of Agriculture and Consumer Economics, University of Illinois (8 March 2013): http://farmdocdaily.illinois.edu/2013/03/exploding-ethanol-rins-prices.html.

Prices vary according to the type of RIN. As can be seen in **Figure 5.6**, many RINs were trading at historical highs at the time of this writing. Commentators have noted that, although the causes are complex, price increases can be attributed partly to an increased regulatory target for RINs for 2014, which is high relative to current production. As a result of these high prices, the oil industry has increased its efforts to repeal or amend the existing RFS requirements.

Program Design Flaws. Unfortunately, because of a design flaw, the RIN trading program has been the victim of several instances of fraud, mainly in the form of RINs being sold but never actually delivered to the buyer. This fraud is possible because of the lack of a centralized authority for the verification and monitoring of RINs. Although the EPA now maintains the Central Data Exchange, it only tracks RINs and is not responsible for their authentication. This situation has allowed sellers to simply create false RINs and post them for sale. One of the worst episodes of fraud occurred in 2012 when the CEO of Absolute Fuels was arrested for selling more than $50 million in counterfeit RINs. Several industry-led efforts are under way to correct the problem. These efforts have resulted in the release of proposed rules as part of the 2013 RFS.[103]

The design flaws and instances of fraud demonstrate that markets need to be developed and monitored carefully. The EPA has begun to address this need by approving voluntary "quality assurance programs" that, if used, will make submitting invalid RINs to the EPA far more difficult than in the past.

Investment Opportunities in RINs. At present, the opportunity to invest directly in RINs is limited, primarily because of the risk of purchasing fraudulent RINs. Exchanges do, however, offer cash-settled RIN contracts, which provide a safe route for investing in RINs without taking actual ownership. Until the EPA or an outside party that is commonly recognized by the major RIN market participants creates an acceptable verification and registration program, purchasing RINs outright will remain risky.

The stock of listed ethanol, biodiesel, or oil-refining companies is also available for purchase, but these companies provide little exposure to the RIN market.

Conclusion. Policymakers have engaged in a variety of efforts over the years to limit US dependence on fossil fuels and foreign oil. The RFS and the RIN program are among the more recent efforts. RINs are used by obligated parties—primarily oil refiners—to ensure compliance with the Renewable

---

[103]EPA proposals can be found here: www.epa.gov/otaq/fuels/renewablefuels/regulations.htm.

Fuel Standard, which mandates levels of renewable fuels to be used in transportation. The RFS has come under scrutiny for promoting ethanol production, which is often viewed as uneconomical and a driver of increases in the price of food, including (but not limited to) the corn used to produce ethanol. A rise in corn prices is an especially severe problem in poor countries and communities that depend on corn for a large part of their nutrition. A rise in corn prices also causes increases in the prices of other foodstuffs.

Although the RIN program is in a state of turmoil because of fraudulent RIN transactions, the program can be a success, in the sense that a market has been established, if the EPA is able to establish a reliable verification and registration system, even if the environmental benefits of the RIN program are still up for debate. One reason for this rosy outlook is the long-dated nature of the program's enabling legislation, the RFS. Many environmental markets are plagued by short-term programs or frequent policy disruptions, but the RFS is established through 2022. Therefore, market participants have sufficient time to properly incorporate the impact of the RFS into their decision-making processes.

Energy Efficiency

Energy efficiency, defined broadly, is the amount of energy required to provide a good or service, and an improvement in energy efficiency is a decrease in that required amount. Often, people think of energy-efficiency improvements in the context of their own homes—exchanging an incandescent light bulb for a compact fluorescent, adding extra insulation, or simply turning down the thermostat. Although these activities may seem mundane, they actually represent an enormous financial opportunity, not only for individual homeowners but also for companies and portfolio managers. This section reviews various categories of energy-efficiency opportunities, discusses the overall impact that energy efficiency can have on the US and world economies and the environment, and explores investment opportunities in energy efficiency.

Energy-efficiency markets are generally not tradable, with the exception of a few states that have incorporated energy-efficiency credits into their renewable portfolio or alternative energy standards or quality assurance programs. Even where energy efficiency is not directly tradable, however, it does affect other tradable markets by altering the supply-and-demand balance in related markets, such as the carbon dioxide and sulfur dioxide markets. As seen in Chapter 4 on the CO_2 markets, an increase in energy efficiency can reduce demand for power or transportation fuels. This effect, in turn, decreases demand for the credits associated with power production, such as RECs and SO2 credits.

Overview and Applications of Energy Efficiency. A common saying in the energy-efficiency field is that the cheapest form of energy is the energy you never use. Amory Lovins, the environmental scientist who founded the Rocky Mountain Institute and pioneered many ideas related to energy efficiency, coined the term "negawatt" to express the idea of a unit of energy saved as a result of energy conservation and efficiency.[104] To illustrate the vast scale at which energy-efficiency upgrades can operate, Lovins concluded that the 39% drop in US energy intensity between 1975 and 2000 effectively represented an energy source 1.7 times the size of all US oil consumption. In fact, energy intensity in the United States has been declining steadily since World War II, as illustrated in **Figure 5.7**. In 2009, McKinsey & Company estimated that the gross energy savings from implementing all of the available profitable energy-efficiency opportunities would yield gross energy savings worth more than $1.2 trillion.[105]

Energy efficiency generally takes place in four sectors: the residential, commercial, industrial, and automotive sectors. The following discussion is

---

[104]Amory Lovins, "The Negawatt Revolution: Solving the CO_2 Problem." Keynote Address at the Green Energy Conference, Montreal (1989): www.ccnr.org/amory.html.
[105]McKinsey & Company, "Unlocking Energy Efficiency in the US Economy," McKinsey & Company (July 2009): www.mckinsey.com/client_service/electric_power_and_natural_gas/latest_thinking/unlocking_energy_efficiency_in_the_us_economy.

Figure 5.7. US Energy Intensity, 1850–2006

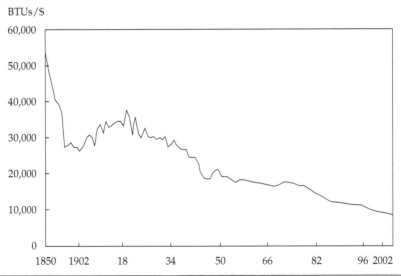

Source: Lester Lave, "The Potential of Energy Efficiency: An Overview," *The Bridge*, vol. 39, no. 2 (Summer 2009):5–14.

focused on the first three of these sectors because the topic of energy efficiency in the automotive sector is widely covered in other publications.[106]

US Residential Sector. With some 115 million residences in the United States, the potential scale of the energy savings opportunities in this sector is huge. According to the DOE, residential buildings consume 22% of the nation's total energy. Some 60% of this energy is used for heating, cooling, refrigeration, and lighting. According to McKinsey & Company, if all residences implemented the energy-efficiency measures with a positive net present value (NPV) for the consumer, the US residential sector would reduce its energy consumption by 28% and save the economy approximately $41 billion annually. (McKinsey estimates the upfront investment of such an effort at $229 billion, yielding a savings of $395 billion in present value terms.)[107]

Appliances represent one of the largest areas of improvement in terms of energy efficiency over the past several decades. Refrigerators, for example, now use about the same amount of electricity per year that they used in 1947, despite the fact that they are now approximately four times larger.

Residential energy-efficiency improvement opportunities can be found both inside the home and outside the building "envelope," as it is often called. Improvements to the exterior of the building might include adding insulation, replacing old windows with newer and more efficient models, sealing duct work, and so forth. Interior improvements typically involve technology changes, such as switching to high-efficiency air conditioners, furnaces, and water heaters, improving lighting design, and replacing old appliances with high-efficiency models. A summary of the savings is shown in **Figure 5.8**.

Although the potential for cost-effective improvements is large, the most important factor in getting them implemented is changing occupants' behavior. Studies show that residents tend to respond to behavior-based energy-efficiency programs. These programs can incorporate data for individual homes that compare residents with their neighbors and provide a goal for energy reduction along with benchmarking. The programs can also be augmented by devices and meters that provide residents with more data about their energy consumption and advice on reducing energy use.

US Commercial and Industrial Sector. The US commercial sector (offices, retail buildings, and so on) consumes almost one-fifth of end-use energy, whereas the industrial sector (light and heavy industry) consumes approximately one-third. McKinsey estimates that if the commercial sector

---

[106]For example, see Amory Lovins, Kyle Datta, Odd-Even Bustnes, Jonathan Koomey, and Nate Glasgow, *Winning the Oil Endgame* (Snowmass, CO: Rocky Mountain Institute, 2004): www.rmi.org/Knowledge-Center/Library/E04-07_WinningTheOilEndgame.
[107]McKinsey, "Unlocking Energy Efficiency," op cit.

Figure 5.8.   Potential for Energy Savings from Residential Products

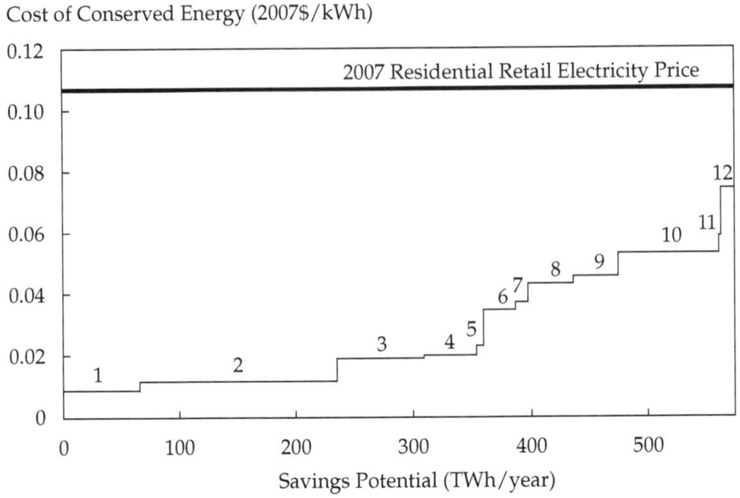

Cost of Conserved Energy (2007$/kWh)

1. Color Television 2. Lighting 3. Other Uses 4. Water Heating
5. Clothes Washer 6. Space Heating 7. Furnace Fan 8. Personal Computer
9. Refrigeration 10. Space Cooling 11. Dishwasher 12. Freezer

Note: kWh = kilowatt-hours; TWh = terawatt-hours.

Source: National Academy of Sciences, National Academy of Engineering, and National Research Council, "Real Prospects for Energy Efficiency in the United States," National Academies Press (2009): www.nae.edu/19582/reports/24921.aspx.

implemented all of the available positive-NPV efficiency improvements, energy consumption in 2020 would be reduced by 29%. The initial investment for these improvements would cost approximately $125 billion and yield a savings of $290 billion.[108]

In some respects, energy-efficiency upgrades in commercial and industrial operations are similar to those in the residential sector. Heating, cooling, and lighting—all play a large role, particularly in the commercial sector. Industrial energy-efficiency improvements, however, often look quite different. Industry uses a wide variety of fuel types, including natural gas; petroleum fuels, such as diesel and fuel oil; and electricity. Although these needs create a more complex energy picture, they provide opportunities for efficient energy generation, such as combined heat and power systems, that often do not exist in commercial or residential settings. Additionally, industry can implement such improvements as converting traditional electric motors, which run at a constant speed, to variable-speed motors that allow for reduced energy use when the full power of the motor is not required.

---

[108]McKinsey, "Unlocking Energy Efficiency," op cit.

Barriers to Implementation and Opportunities for Innovation.
If improvement in energy efficiency is such a large opportunity, why aren't more people taking advantage of it? The answer is that there are a lot of barriers to implementation of energy efficiency.

One barrier to implementation is the uncertainty surrounding the level of actual energy savings to be expected. Many of the gains from energy-efficiency measures are based on estimates. These estimates assume certain usage patterns and other behavior that can fluctuate heavily among users. Actual savings may be above or below the estimates, but the risk of investing the necessary capital to make the improvement and not realizing the anticipated gain from reduced energy consumption makes energy efficiency a riskier investment than it would otherwise be.

Many states have energy-efficiency mandates. In most cases, these mandates require electric utilities to implement energy-efficiency programs for their customers. The mandates and the programs they require entail a complex set of critical points with many nuances. The discussion here is limited to a short list of the most relevant points.

Given that the primary business and route to profitability for most electric utilities is producing and selling power, requiring electric utilities to implement programs that motivate customers to purchase less power is a less-than-ideal incentive structure. Some states have given utilities greater incentives to invest in customer energy efficiency by providing, through the regulated rate-making process, a return on the utility's investment in "demand management" (the term of art for exhorting customers to buy less of the utility's product). Perhaps if more policymakers adopted similar policies, or provided incentives directly to consumers instead of penalizing power producers who do not comply with state mandates, a more widespread adoption of energy efficiency would occur.

Additionally, the structure of electricity purchases is not conducive to promoting energy efficiency. Electricity bills are normally paid at the end of the month, after the electricity has been used. Monitoring and displaying power consumption in a more real-time way would probably generate increased interest in saving energy.

Other barriers have less to do with information availability and personal finance and more to do with human behavior and a lack of focus on energy consumption. Old habits are often hard to break. Turning the lights off when you leave the room is easy enough to do. But if you are not focused on energy consumption, you often leave the lights on. This lack of attention paid to energy use exists not only in homes but also in corporate settings. Some companies assume that their energy bills and their level of energy consumption are unavoidable costs of doing business. As energy prices have increased, however, and new companies have formed to help others reduce their energy use, traditional attitudes about energy use have begun to change. Each of these barriers has become an opportunity for the companies that will be listed in the next section.

Investment Opportunities in US Energy Efficiency. Energy efficiency presents a wide variety of investment opportunities. To simplify the discussion, we break the opportunities into four primary areas: utility and energy companies, energy-efficiency service providers, equipment vendors, and energy-efficiency financiers.

▨ *Utility and energy companies.* Among the largest players in the industry are utilities based in states with strong energy-efficiency mandates, including California, Connecticut, and Massachusetts, which have had such mandates for a number of years. Major players include the utilities Sempra Energy (NYSE: SRE), Pacific Gas and Electric (NYSE: PCG), Constellation Energy (NYSE: CEG), and Con Edison (NYSE: ED).

▨ *Service providers.* Energy-efficiency service providers include engineering firms, consultants, energy-efficiency monitoring companies, energy service companies, and others. Major players are Ameresco (NYSE: AMRC), Johnson Controls (NYSE: JCI), Schneider Electric (EPA: SU), Siemens (NYSE: SI), Honeywell (NYSE: HON), EnerNOC (NASDAQ: ENOC), and Trane (NYSE: IR).

▨ *Equipment vendors.* Equipment vendors typically provide parts for building automation and control as well as demand response. Major players include Johnson Controls, Carrier (part of United Technologies, NYSE: UTX), Cisco Systems (NASDAQ: CSCO), KMC Controls (private), Lutron Electronics (private), and Siemens.

▨ *Funding sources.* Funders can vary from for-profit companies (such as banks) to private equity funds, project finance groups, and philanthropic foundations. Major players include Bank of America (NYSE: BAC), GE Capital (NYSE: GE), Johnson Controls, Forsyth Street Advisors (private), Pegasus Capital Advisors (private), and Living Cities.

Tradable Energy-Efficiency Markets. As with the other functioning emissions markets, trading in energy efficiency requires the creation of property rights. In this case, some form of tradable instrument is needed that verifies that the energy-efficiency goal has been achieved. The integrity of these property rights should be verified by a designated third party, and a registry should be set up to transfer and track the property rights. This section will give a few examples of tradable energy-efficiency markets outside the United States.

▨ *India.* The Perform, Achieve and Trade program is essentially a cap-and-trade program aimed at reducing energy consumption and improving energy efficiency in industries across India. The scheme is being designed and implemented by the Bureau of Energy Efficiency in India's Ministry of Power. It is designed to set benchmark efficiency levels for 563 big polluters, such as power plants, steel mills, and cement plants. These emitters account for 54% of the country's energy consumption. Under this program, entities that need to use more energy than mandated will be required to buy tradable energy saving certificates (ESCerts). Similarly, entities that use less energy can sell their ESCerts. The number of ESCerts will depend on the amount of energy saved in a target year. The government estimates that this market will be worth $16 billion in 2014, when trading is to begin.

▧ *Europe.* As can be seen in **Table 5.3**, several European countries have already implemented a marketplace for energy-efficiency credits, whereas others are still exploring it. The basic idea is the same in each of the countries presented in the table: Energy savings will be verified by a designated regulator and will be represented by so-called white certificates (tradable certificates for energy savings). In Italy, the certificates are called "energy efficiency titles," and trading began in 2005.

Conclusion

Energy efficiency provides many rewarding opportunities, in terms of investment as well as energy reduction and environmental gain. The biggest obstacles to large-scale implementation are behavioral and financial. Innovative companies are beginning to address these barriers in interesting ways. Corporations, together with individual homeowners, are beginning to realize the importance of good energy management and the savings potential of energy-efficient upgrades in lighting, heating, cooling, and related activities.

In this chapter, we explored environmental markets that put prices on renewable energy, renewable identification numbers, and energy efficiency. Given the policy debate regarding climate change and the use of fossil fuels, the emergence of such markets is timely. The use of renewable energy, RINs, and the promotion of energy efficiencies—all help to lower dependence on fossil fuels.

One other environmental asset that is closely intertwined with energy use and, therefore, part of the equation is water. And it is the topic of the next chapter. The water–energy nexus is the need for water to produce energy and energy to produce water. Water is a critical input for producing conventional energy because it is used to cool steam turbines. It is also used in refining transportation fuels; extracting some fuels, such as coal and petroleum; and growing biofuel crops. Similarly, the water we use needs energy for its extraction, transportation, and purification. The use of renewable energy and energy-efficient appliances saves both energy and water. Similarly, using renewable energy technologies, such as wind and solar, enables us to eliminate the use of water for electricity production from these sources.

Table 5.3. Energy-Efficiency Commitment in the United Kingdom, Italy, and France

United Kingdom (EEC-2, 2005–2008)	Italy	France (planned)
Driver		
Quota system	Quota system	Quota system
• TWh fuel–weighted energy benefits	• Ton of oil equivalent	• TWh
• 2005–2008	• Annual 2005–2009	• 2006–2008 (first period)
• Projects targeted toward domestic consumers only	• Projects targeted at all consumers	• Projects targeted at all consumers
• 50% from "priority group" (low-income consumers on social benefits)	• 50% from reduction in own energy vector (electricity and gas)	
Obliged parties		
• Electricity and gas suppliers	• Electricity and gas distributors	• Electricity, gas, liquefied petroleum gas, heat, cold and heating fuel suppliers
Obligation threshold and apportionment criteria		
• Threshold: 50,000 domestic customers served	• Threshold: 100,000 customers served	• Threshold: 0.4 TWh/ year of energy sales
• Reference parameter for apportionment: number of domestic consumers served	• Reference parameter for apportionment: electricity/gas distributed (market share)	• Reference parameter for apportionment: market shares and energy sales turnover on residential and tertiary sectors
• In EEC-1: Progressively tighter for companies with more customers; no longer progressively tighter targets in EEC-2	• Linear (i.e., the targets get tighter linearly as opposed to some other way)	
Trading		
• No certificates	• Certificates trade	• Certificates trade, only bilateral exchanges
• Obligations can be traded	• Spot market sessions	
• Savings can be traded but only after own obligation has been met	• OTC trading	
• Approval from regulator	• Rules approved by the regulator	
• No spot market		
• One-way trade in national emissions-trading scheme possible in principle		

Table 5.3.   Energy-Efficiency Commitment in the United Kingdom, Italy, and France (continued)

United Kingdom (EEC-2, 2005–2008)	Italy	France (planned)
Cost recovery		
• No fixed cost recovery; suppliers may include costs in the electricity/gas end-user's price; the reason is the competitive nature of supply; suppliers are not constrained by customer or measure type as to how to recover costs	• Only for own energy vector; allowed for customers of another distributor • Determined *ex ante* by the regulator: standard average lump sum (maximum allowed costs)	• Rise in prices and tariffs to be limited to maximum 0.5% of the consumer bill
Penalty		
• The regulator can consider whether it is appropriate to set a penalty • No specific guidance on how penalty would be calculated • The penalty can reach up to 10% of the supplier's turnover	• "Proportional and in any case greater than investments needed to compensate for noncompliance" • Fixed by the regulator	• 0.02 euro/kWh

Note: EEC is engery-efficiency commitment.

Source: EEA, "Market-Based Instruments for Environmental Policy in Europe," European Environmental Agency technical report (August 2005).

6. Water Markets and Associated Asset Classes

Water promises to be the most important commodity of the 21st century. Global water demand is rising faster than at any other time in human history. Supplies of water, an already scarce resource and one with no substitute, are declining because of decreasing snow cover and increasing drought. In light of these significant challenges, water must be properly conserved.

The social, economic, and environmental consequences of the water challenge are enormous. Water is an essential ingredient for life sustenance, food production, and energy production. Most manufacturing and production activities have implications for the water supply because they use water both directly as an input and indirectly through energy consumption. Because 22% of global gross domestic product (GDP) comes from regions where water is scarce, the growth-limiting concerns from water scarcity are critical.

From a social standpoint, the estimate is that more than 1 billion people lack access to a safe water supply and close to 2.5 billion people lack access to proper sanitation. In developing countries, 80% of all childhood illnesses and deaths are directly or indirectly caused by unsanitary water.

The purpose of this chapter is to describe how these problems of water shortages and quality are being and can be addressed. Pricing both the rights to use water and the rights to pollute it can achieve social objectives and provide commercial opportunities to the financial and industrial sectors of countries.

Background

Even though we live on a planet whose surface is more than 70% covered with water, little of that water is available for consumption. Only 2.5% of the global water supply is freshwater, and the majority of it is locked away in glaciers, snow cover, and deep underground aquifers. Only 1% of freshwater is readily available for human and animal use.[109] Therefore, much less than 1/10 of 1% of all the water on Earth is readily available for consumption. (For the purposes of this chapter, "freshwater" is defined as water containing minimal amounts of salt—that is, water from rivers, lakes, and aquifers; "clean water" is defined as water suitable for drinking and is a subset of freshwater.)[110]

In addition, this available supply is unevenly distributed across the world. North and South America and Europe generally have sufficient quantities of

---

[109]USGS, "The World's Water," US Geological Survey, Water Science School (last modified 5 November 2013): http://ga.water.usgs.gov/edu/earthwherewater.html.
[110]US Geological Survey: http://ga.water.usgs.gov/edu/watercyclefreshstorage.html.

water, whereas parts of China and India, the Middle East, and many parts of Africa are woefully and increasingly short of it. Consider North America versus China. North America has only 8% of the world's population, but it has 15% of the freshwater on Earth. China, in contrast, has 21% of the population but only 7% of the available freshwater.[111] Such imbalances as these, coupled with the fact that many of the world's water basins cross national boundaries, create a recipe for geopolitical conflict and cross-border tension.

Like the water supply, the demand for water is uneven across the world. In regions of water abundance, either real or perceived, multiple contributing factors have led to an unsustainable and injudicious use of the resource. For example, the per capita water footprint in the United States is 1,797 gallons per day. In South America, it is 341 gallons per day. And the world average is about 897 gallons per day.[112] On a residential basis, Americans use 100–150 gallons of water per day per person. The average European uses 74 gallons, and the average Chinese uses 23 gallons.[113]

The per capita water requirement for basic human needs, such as drinking, hygiene, sanitation, and food preparation, is about 15 gallons per day. Some of this demand is triggered by population growth. On a global basis, however, water demand doubles every 20 years, despite a population growth rate of less than half that. Increased water consumption is also driven by increased standards of living. This fact is particularly relevant for such countries as China and India, where millions of people continue to move from rural to urban areas. It is also of interest to the newest group of Asian countries attracting interest from financiers and industrial companies: Malaysia, Indonesia, the Philippines, and Singapore (the MIPS). Like much of the rest of the world, these countries suffer from water imbalances.

The MIPS are exceptionally attractive from an investment standpoint because of their prospects for growth. Singapore, in particular, with its favorable political climate, is uniquely positioned as a financial hub. Because of its geographical location, Singapore is naturally short of water and has been meeting its water needs by importing water from Malaysia, investing in water technology, and building capital-intensive water infrastructure. Malaysia has had abundant water historically but is now facing scarcity as a result of water mismanagement. The two countries are engaged in a long-standing conflict over water supply.

---

[111]Deane Dray, Adam Samuelson, Mark Zepf, and Ajay Kejriwal, "The Essentials of Investing in the Water Sector, Version 2.0," Goldman Sachs Global Investment Research (24 March 2008): www.slideshare.net/Water_Food_Energy_Nexus/goldman-sachs-the-essentials-of-investing-in-the-water-sector.

[112]National Water Footprint Calculator, Water Footprint Network (2012): www.waterfootprint.org/?page=cal/waterfootprintcalculator_national.

[113]Peter H. Gleick, "Basic Water Requirements for Human Activities: Meeting Basic Needs," *Water International*, vol. 21, no. 2 (1996):83–92.

Although Indonesia has access to 21% of the total freshwater available in the Asia-Pacific region, its rapid development and poor infrastructure have led to increasing water scarcity. The country also has undergone significant land-use changes, and deforestation and extractive industries have left many areas more vulnerable than in the past to such extreme events as monsoon floods. In 2010, less than half the total population lacked access to safe water and a quarter of the population had access to piped water.[114]

In the Philippines, access to clean water is a serious problem. Waterborne diseases cause 55 deaths a day and $1.56 billion worth of economic losses annually.

The water crisis involves not only quantity but also, and of equal importance, water quality. These two issues are closely related. Such nutrients as nitrogen and phosphorus occur naturally as contaminants in water, soil, and air. Moreover, nitrogen and phosphorus in fertilizer aid the growth of agricultural crops. But the excessive presence of nutrients in watersheds can have harmful consequences. Exposure to excessive levels of nitrate (a form of nitrogen) can reduce oxygen levels in blood, putting infants, children, and adults with lung or cardiovascular disease at increased health risk. Research has also linked long-term consumption of excess nitrates to cancer.

Poor water quality is an issue not only for humans but also for wildlife. High concentrations of phosphorus or ammonia in lakes, streams, and reservoirs are often responsible for fish mortality, foul odors, and excessive aquatic weed growth.

Water pollution sources can be divided into two types. *Point sources* are those that can be attributed to a specific physical location—such as power plants or refineries, which are often located near rivers and lakes for cooling and shipping purposes—and nutrient discharges from wastewater-treatment plants, industries, or municipalities. *Nonpoint sources*—the main cause of nutrient pollution—are diffuse sources of pollution, pollution that cannot be attributed to a clearly identified, specific physical location or a defined discharge channel. Such pollution includes the nutrients that run off the ground from any land use—croplands, lawns, parking lots, streets, forests, and so on—and enter waterways. This source also includes nutrients that enter water through air pollution, through groundwater, or from septic systems.

The supply-and-demand imbalance of freshwater is not just a major concern for the health and well-being of the population; it also has massive implications for finance and business. The global water industry is estimated

---

[114]"Indonesia Water Investment Roadmap 2011–2014," World Bank: http://water.worldbank.org/sites/water.worldbank.org/files/publication/WATER-Indonesia-Water-Investment-Roadmap-2011-2014.pdf.

to be valued at $500 billion, an amount that could double by 2030–2035.[115] Annual capital expenditures on water infrastructure alone could grow from their 2010 level of $90 billion to $131 billion in 2016. Global annual investment in wastewater-treatment equipment is expected to rise from $14 billion in 2010 to $22 billion in 2016.[116]

With demand for water outpacing supply by 40%, water scarcity is likely to become as big a policy issue by 2030 as oil scarcity is today. This situation presents a massive opportunity for investors and analysts in the areas of desalination, "smart" water meters, efficient irrigation technologies, wastewater treatment, infrastructure, engineering, and other water-related businesses. The desalination industry alone is projected to be worth as much as $25 billion by 2025. Estimates suggest that annual water investment needs for the Organisation for Economic Co-Operation and Development (OECD) countries and the BRICs (Brazil, Russia, India, and China) will rise to more than $770 billion by 2015.[117] Without investment in water-related products, services, and infrastructure, 45% of projected global GDP in 2050 could be at risk. (This percentage amounts to $63 trillion in 2000 prices.) The economic sectors most affected are likely to be those that rely heavily on water: utilities, oil and gas, mining, food and beverages, and cosmetics.[118]

Growing Demand for a Finite Resource

Demand for water is being driven by population growth, rising agricultural needs, urbanization, and growing energy demand.

Agriculture. The challenges agriculture faces, even without taking into account issues of water scarcity, are daunting. The OECD estimates that the world will need to produce almost 50% more food than is produced today by 2030 to meet increased demand and population growth.[119]

The imbalance between water supply and demand in agriculture stems from two factors: (1) waste, primarily through irrigation losses, and (2) subsidies and the lack of proper water pricing. Agriculture consumes about 70% of the world's freshwater *withdrawals* (that is, extractions from a freshwater resource, such as a river, lake, or aquifer), and agriculture is also one of the primary causes

---

[115]Sarbjit Nahal, Valery Lucas-Leclin, Julie Dolle, and John King, "The Global Water Sector," Bank of America/Merrill Lynch Wealth Management (28 September 2011).

[116]Jablanka Uzelac, Ankit Patel, and Heather Lang, *Global Water Market 2011: Financing the World's Water Needs until 2016* (Oxford, UK: Media Analytics, 2010).

[117]The OECD consists of 34 mostly developed countries and was founded in 1961 to stimulate economic progress and world trade.

[118]Nahal et al., "The Global Water Sector," op cit.

[119]Water Law Research Guide, Georgetown Law Library: www.law.georgetown.edu/library/research/guides/waterlaw.cfm.

of nonpoint source pollution and water contamination. Moreover, most of the water withdrawn is *consumed*; little is returned to its source.

In the United States, for example, water used for irrigation and livestock makes up about 31% of water withdrawals, and because so little agricultural water is returned to its source (unlike water for electricity generation), agriculture makes up 85% of US water consumption. This circumstance presents a massive opportunity for companies working on reducing losses from irrigation and other agricultural uses. By reducing just 15%–20% of the water consumed by irrigated agriculture, we could largely alleviate water scarcity globally.[120] Later in this chapter, we discuss specific opportunities.

Additionally, property rights for water are often allocated in ways that introduce inefficiencies into the market. In the western United States, agricultural users have senior rights, even though they may add less value per unit of water than other users. Thus, an opportunity for gains from trade in water rights exists.

Agriculture's role as the primary nonpoint source of pollution and a leading source of water contamination comes from the excess application of pesticides, poor management of animal feeding and grazing operations, excessive plowing, and improper irrigation techniques. All of these practices contribute to nonpoint source pollution through excess nutrients in surface and groundwater bodies, sediment runoff, the buildup of metals and salts, and the introduction of pathogens.

Some insight into agriculture's impact on water use can be gained by considering the volume of water embedded in the food we consume.[121] A pound of corn requires 55 gallons of water. Similarly, a pound of wheat requires 156 gallons of water. These quantities may not seem like a lot, but remember that most of the corn produced is eventually fed to beef cattle. For this reason, increased meat consumption is a primary driver of the growing demand for water from agriculture. Beef, in particular, requires a large amount of water to produce. Producing a pound of beef is estimated to require 1,857 gallons of water.

A gallon of milk requires 880 gallons of water, and a pound of pork requires 756 gallons. Contrast these requirements with what fruits and vegetables require: a pound of oranges requires only 55 gallons of water.

This difference is one reason water use tends to increase as incomes increase: Rising incomes generally lead to increases in meat consumption.

---

[120]Brian D. Richter, David Abell, Emily Bacha, Kate Brauman, Stavros Calos, Alex Cohn, Carlos Disla, Sarah Friedlander O'Brien, David Hodges, Scott Kaiser, Maria Loughran, Cristina Mestre, Melissa Reardon, and Emma Siegfried, "Tapped Out: How Can Cities Secure Their Water Future?" *Water Policy*, vol. 15, no. 3:335–363.

[121]The source of these data is the Water Footprint Network: www.waterfootprint.org.

Diet upgrades in developing countries, therefore—if those consumers follow the same diet patterns observed in the United States and Europe—have the potential to dramatically increase water demand.

Urbanization. According to the United Nations, urban areas will house approximately 60% of the global population by 2030.[122] In 2007, the world for the first time in its history had more urban dwellers than rural. Unfortunately, many of these urban dwellers, particularly the poor, lack access to safe drinking water and sanitation. As a result, such diseases as diarrhea, malaria, and cholera are common in some urban areas. The estimate is that urbanization leads to a fivefold increase in water demand beyond the basic requirements of drinking, cleaning, and sanitation.

Energy. Production of energy requires a significant quantity of water and also has an impact on water quality. Water is an important ingredient for cooling steam electric power plants and is required to generate hydropower. Water is also used in extracting, refining, and producing petroleum fuels; growing biofuel crops; and hydraulic fracking for natural gas. Similarly, a lot of energy is consumed in treating and transporting water for consumption and for industrial and irrigation purposes. Given the strength of this water–energy nexus, one can infer that a water shortage can inhibit energy production—a problem that may be exacerbated by an increased demand for electricity.

According to the International Energy Agency (IEA), the amount of freshwater consumed for energy production may double in the next 25 years (from 66 billion cubic meters [bcm] annually today to 135 bcm). In the United States, power plants withdraw 143 billion gallons of freshwater daily, more than the amount withdrawn for irrigation and three times as much as is used for public water supplies. Unlike most other water withdrawals, however, the vast majority of water withdrawals for power production and urban use are returned to the source after use.[123]

Decreasing Supply

Whether or not climate change is anthropogenic, the effects of a changing climate and water stress are clearly now marching forward hand in hand. With extreme weather events and patterns being observed with increasing

---

[122]Information in this paragraph comes largely from "Global Themes Strategy: Thirsty Cities—Urbanization to Drive Water Demand," Citi Thematic Investing Research (20 July 2011): http://fa.smithbarney.com/public/projectfiles/f8e732d5-6162-4cd9-8b1d-7b7317360163.pdf. Accessed 21 May 2013.

[123]Data in this paragraph come from "World Energy Outlook 2012," International Energy Agency: www.worldenergyoutlook.org/publications/weo-2012/.

frequency, questions regarding the impact of the changing climate on the water supply are becoming commonplace. The UN Convention to Combat Desertification estimates that roughly a third of the land surface of the planet is now turning to desert land and that the affected area is growing by more than 5 million hectares annually.[124] Much like the distribution of water, the impact of climate change on the water supply varies significantly by location. Australia and parts of the United States are experiencing record droughts and diminished snow pack, whereas some tropical regions are experiencing large increases in rainfall, mudslides, and runoff.

Water Pricing and Subsidies

Among the many reasons the world has arrived at its current water crisis, perhaps none is more important than lack of a proper price for water itself. The mispricing of scarce resources has been shown, time and again, to result in suboptimal allocation of those resources. Prices for the delivery of water in Chicago and New York are roughly $0.002 and $0.004 per gallon, respectively.[125] The price of water in New Delhi is only a fifth of the cost of delivering it.[126] These prices do not even take into account the cost of the water itself, which is essentially viewed as a free and unlimited resource. The US government subsidizes more than half the cost of water and wastewater systems. Researchers also estimate that US farmers would pay roughly 25% more if water for agricultural use were unsubsidized. Unfortunately, such mispricing of water is not uncommon, and it leads to increased demand and misallocation of resources.

Budget constraints do, however, put pressure on politicians to reduce water subsidies. This confluence of factors is likely to become increasingly relevant for investors and analysts. As subsidies diminish, changes in consumption are sure to follow on both the industrial and residential levels. These changes may mean new opportunities for smart water meters; advanced leak detection equipment; changes in practices in water-intensive industries, such as semiconductor manufacturing; and, of course, changes in agriculture.[127]

It is important to emphasize that this discussion of pricing only applies to water consumption above and beyond the amount needed for basic hydration and hygiene purposes.

---

[124]One square mile is roughly 259 hectares.

[125]The source for Chicago prices is Whet Moser, "Chicago's Proposed Water Rate Hike: At What Cost?" *Chicago* magazine (14 October 2011). The source for New York City comes from the rate schedule effective 1 July 2012, NYC Water Board.

[126]Nahal et al., "The Global Water Sector," op cit.

[127]Dray et al., "The Essentials of Investing in the Water Sector," op cit.

Solutions to the Supply–Demand Imbalance: The Role of Trading

Driven by economic growth and increasing agricultural withdrawals, global water demand is expected to grow from about 4,500 bcm to 6,900 bcm by 2030. The historical solution for meeting water demand has been to increase supply though large infrastructure projects and technological solutions. They include more inventory and delivery infrastructure, such as dams and canals, and increased technology supply, such as desalination plants. Such large-scale projects are usually expensive, time intensive, and disruptive to the ecosystem and local communities. With water pricing and defined resource rights, however, a number of measures that enhance efficient use of water become viable, can be deployed quickly, and may be cheaper than the traditional technological solutions. Such measures as irrigation scheduling, wastewater reuse, and enhanced efficiency of industrial water use can be "low-hanging fruit" solutions that merit attention.

A water-trading program that facilitates pricing and transferability of water rights provides the incentives to initiate such low-cost measures. In addition, water pricing can drive consumers to put water to its most valuable and highest use.

Because water is a local or regional resource, local availability, supply-and-demand characteristics, and environmental stress will play important roles in determining which strategies are best. Trading can expand the options available beyond purely local ones, however, as can be seen historically with acid rain pollutants and carbon dioxide. For example, desalination technology, a much-talked-about technological solution to meeting freshwater demands, costs on average $650–$2,200 per acre-foot (the volume of 1 acre of surface area to the depth of 1 foot, or about 326,000 gallons). In comparison, optimal irrigation scheduling can provide net savings of $24–$148 per acre-foot and such industrial measures as changing to paste tailing in mining can provide net savings of $370–$740 per acre-foot.[128] Whenever diverse options with varying abatement costs exist, trading mechanisms like those described in this book provide the lowest-cost solutions and, therefore, highest social gains.

One example involves the investment decision facing the city of Adelaide in South Australia. The Adelaide government faced the task of meeting city water demand. The decision involved building desalination capacity of 100 gigaliters (GL) per year versus purchasing an equivalent amount of high-reliability Victorian Murray (VM) entitlements.[129] The project involved capital

---

[128]Tailings are the materials left over after the valuable parts have been separated from the uneconomic parts of an ore. Paste tailings are tailings that have been significantly dewatered.
[129]One gigaliter is 810.7 acre-feet. The Victorian Murray catchment is the basin of the Murray River in the state of Victoria. The term "high reliability" is explained later in this chapter.

expenditures of AU$1.83 billion and operating costs at full capacity of AU$130 million annually, or AU$0.005 per gallon. The trading alternative involving the high-reliability VM entitlements would cost AU$190 million, with operating costs between AU$0.0008 and AU$0.0010 per gallon.[130] Clearly, the trading option was cheaper from the standpoints of capital expenditures and operating costs. In addition, the trading option ensured flexibility because in good years, any unused entitlements could be sold to other market participants.

Another example involves meeting water demand for the southern Indian city of Chennai.[131] The city faced chronic water shortages that forced rationing of water for residents and closed factories because of lack of water. Aided by a lack of regulation governing groundwater, the common technological solution involved sinking deep tube wells in which 100–200 mm (5–8 inch) wide stainless steel tubes or pipes are bored into an underground aquifer. This solution soon becomes futile, however, because groundwater levels drop and sea saltwater intrudes on the aquifer. The local government, together with the World Bank, conducted a feasibility study in 1996 to weigh other solutions. The technological alternative, the Veeranam project, involved piping water 155 miles to the city and included a desalination plant. The trading alternative involved buying water entitlements from rice farmers in the Araniar-Kortalaiyar (AK) aquifer, which was close to the city. The aquifer was shown to have a sustainable water yield sufficient to meet the city's water demands. As shown in **Table 6.1**, the water-trading option was by far the cheapest option.

City policymakers were not keen on the entitlement option because they feared it would anger the farmers. They believed AK aquifer water was considered an inalienable right by the farmers and that any attempt to export the water to the city would be seen as politically unfavorable. However, the option was reluctantly adopted. In 2003, 70% of the city's water came from buying water entitlements sold by farmers.

---

[130]Based on the February 2011 average price, tendered from Australia's government environmental purchasing program.

[131]*India's Water Economy: Bracing for a Turbulent Future* (Washington, DC: World Bank, 2005): https://openknowledge.worldbank.org/handle/10986/8413.

Table 6.1. Comparative Costs and Quantities of Supplying Water to Chennai

Method	Capacity (gallons per day)	Cost ($ per gallon)
Recycled industrial sewage	6,075,956	$0.0038
AK aquifer water entitlements	59,967,044	0.0001
Veeranam project	11,887,740	0.0009
Desalination unit	26,417,200	0.0034

Notes: This analysis assumes an exchange rate of 55 Indian rupees per US dollar. Recycled industrial sewage costs per gallon are high because of local environmental regulations.

In fact, the farmers *were* upset, but not because their "inalienable right" was being taken away. They were upset because they could not sell all that they wanted to the local water utility.

This story demonstrates that when transferable property rights are properly assigned and price is established, rational actors will optimize the use of a resource. In this case, rice farmers found it more profitable to generate revenues by selling water rights than it would have been to use the water for farming.

Virtual Water: Synthetic Trading. The concept of virtual water is a recent one, but its underlying principle has existed for millennia. Virtual water is a way of expressing the quantity of water embedded in food or other goods that are traded around the globe. The notion of virtual water came about as a way to express the idea that countries with relatively few freshwater resources would be better off outsourcing water-intensive activities to countries with greater freshwater resources. In the absence of functioning markets for water, there is a surrogate for water trading: The global grain trade is, in effect, a virtual water trade, although it is not often referred to as such.

Today, many countries engage in crop production or other water-intensive activities in other countries that have relatively abundant water resources. China, for example, has invested in more than 6 million acres of rice, sugar, maize, and biofuel production in several African countries and the Philippines. Saudi Arabia has invested in more than 5 million acres of rice, wheat, vegetables, and other agricultural production in Sudan, Tanzania, Indonesia, and other countries with available freshwater resources. The UN Environment Programme estimates the trade of virtual water to be roughly 612 trillion gallons (2,320 bcm) per year, with the biggest net importers being the Middle East, North Africa, Mexico, Europe, Japan, and South Korea. The estimate is that without this virtual water trade, the world would have used an additional 92 trillion gallons (352 bcm) annually between 1997 and 2001.[132] Using Chicago's water delivery cost of $0.002 per gallon and the estimated savings of 92 trillion gallons per year, the world saves an estimated $186 billion annually through the virtual water trade.

Water Quality and Quantity Trading. Recall the difference between rights to *pollute* and rights to *use*. Sulfur dioxide, nitrogen oxide, carbon dioxide, and greenhouse gas allowances are all rights to pollute. Water quantity trading is the first example in this book of rights to use; it constitutes the right to use a prespecified amount of a natural resource—in this case, water.

---

[132]M.M. Mekonnen and A.Y. Hoekstra, "National Water Footprints Accounts: The Green, Blue and Grey Water Footprint of Production and Consumption," Value of Water Research Report Series No. 50, UNESCO-IHE (May 2011).

Although some impediments to trading water exist, they are not insurmountable and can be overcome with good contract and market design. Some of the characteristics unique to water as a commodity, to differentiate it from the other environmental assets, are as follows:

- Water is a regional product. It is bulky and costly to move in the volumes typically required for production, so it can be transferred only between neighboring river basins up to about 500 kilometers, or about 0.621 miles (or even shorter distances if it needs to be pumped uphill). Because of this characteristic and the flow of water from upstream to downstream users, risks and responses must be understood on the basis of a river basin, not on a global scale as can be done for carbon.

- Water availability is variable in time and space, and therefore, its short- and long-term future availability is uncertain.

- Water is a finite but renewable resource, the availability of which is physically constrained by the infrastructure in place and legally constrained in many locations by complex historical water rights systems.

- Water is nonsubstitutable in most domestic and productive activities, although it may be more efficiently used.

Despite these unique characteristics, water markets are like all other markets in that they can thrive only in an environment of unambiguous property rights. Much like the institutions that were created for SO2 and CO_2, a market infrastructure is needed for water markets to exist and thrive. Monitoring, verification, product standards, and so forth, are necessary, but the foundation upon which the market framework is built is unambiguous property rights.

The structural changes necessary for the establishment of an organized water market are already under way in many parts of the world. Such design elements as standardization, grading and quantification guidelines, a legal framework that recognizes property rights, proper monitoring and verification procedures, ability to track transfers, and so forth, are all being developed as water markets begin to take shape. Although many of the markets are still in the early stages of development, they provide important proof-of-concept lessons for others considering the use of markets to efficiently manage water quality and quantity.

▨ *Water pollutants trading.* The fundamentals of water trading are quite simple. On the quality side, a cap is typically placed on the amount of pollutant entering the watershed. Much like a cap-and-trade program for GHGs or other environmental commodities, a reduction goal is then established for the pollutant and permits are allocated to the participating (i.e., capped) sources. Once the capped sources have been allocated their permits, they are motivated to reduce their pollutant discharges beyond their reduction targets because they can sell any excess permits that may result. This buying and selling of permits allows the capped sources to take advantage of the lowest-cost opportunities to reduce their levels of pollution.[133]

To give an example, the nitrogen and phosphorus discharges from factories and farms were polluting the Chesapeake Bay by reducing the oxygen level of the water. The result was harmful to the marine ecosystem and human health. In 2005, a nutrient cap-and-trade program was initiated that limited the amount of nutrients flowing into the rivers by issuing "water quality credits" to polluting entities. Various legislative proposals are calling for the system to be expanded. The program could eventually be extended to include fishermen, based on the idea that catches will increase if the bay has fewer "dead zones" caused by oxygen depletion. A 2012 report by the Chesapeake Bay Commission concluded that implementing a watershed-wide cap-and-trade system could result in a cost savings of approximately $1.2 billion annually for entities that are subject to the Environmental Protection Agency's water pollutant regulations.[134]

▨ *Water temperature trading.* Water quality trading can also be based on water temperature, which matters because the aquatic ecosystem—specifically, certain species of fish—can be especially sensitive to sudden changes in water temperature. Thus, water temperature credits were developed to mitigate incidents when factories, power plants, or wastewater-treatment systems release a large amount of warm water into a lake or river. Instead of mandating the installation of expensive water-cooling systems, regulators allow farmers and other landowners to plant trees and other stream bank vegetation to shade streams to cool them down naturally. This practice also improves the animal habitat and provides other environmental benefits. Credits are then issued for cooling the streams and can be sold to regulated entities, such as wastewater-treatment authorities.

The development of creative regional markets regulating riparian water temperature in the western United States to protect local fishery resources serves as a reminder that many environmental outcomes can be achieved through properly designed markets.[135] In 2006, the Oregon Department of Environmental Quality (DEQ) finalized the Willamette River temperature requirements to protect salmon during the spring and autumn when they are spawning and during the summer when they are reaching adulthood and migrating.

---

[133]The World Resources Institute has written extensively on water quality trading: http://pdf.wri.org/water_trading_quality_programs_international_overview.pdf.

[134]"Could Cap and Trade Cut Costs for Water Polluters?" *American Water Intelligence*, vol. 3, no. 6 (June 2012): www.americanwaterintel.com/archive/3/6/general/could-cap-and-trade-cut-costs-water-polluters.html.

[135]The term "riparian" means of, on, or relating to the banks of a natural course of water.

The development of water temperature trading illustrates that markets can help by addressing issues of nutrient loads as well as by playing a role in water quality attributes, such as temperature. This trading may also be important for investors or analysts looking at real estate and agricultural land with surface streams and rivers. Moreover, the reestablishment of stream banks may be a new income source in areas where these markets are in place.[136]

▓ *Water quantity trading.* Water quantity trading is a system whereby the rights to use water are traded. The most mature of these markets are in Australia, which began to establish them in the 1990s because the authorities were worried that farmers were depleting the country's reserves. In 1994, water reforms by the Council of Australian Governments (COAG) enabled the separation of water rights from the land rights.[137] This reform also sought to open up interstate water trading. In 2010, the Australian water market was estimated to be valued at approximately AU$3.1 billion. Similarly, water trading of some kind exists in many states of the western United States as well as in Alberta, Canada. Water exchange systems also exist in South Africa and Chile.

Because the Australian system is the longest-running and most advanced system, we discuss it in detail in this chapter to illustrate the benefits of water quantity trading.

Australian Water Markets

Australia is an arid country. Scarcity is naturally a key concern in many parts of Australia, where long periods of drought threaten the availability of water for agricultural irrigation and the long-term secure drinking supply. Rainfall distribution is geographically uneven and highly seasonal.

Prior to 1970, water rights in Australia were tied to the land. Available water was allocated on a first-come/first-served basis, and the charge (or marginal cost) to users was close to zero. Increases in demand were met through government-funded increases in infrastructure investment, which often were motivated more by politics than by a formal cost–benefit assessment. During droughts, a variety of quantitative regulations were used to ration supplies. These allocation procedures applied for cities and countryside and for surface and underground water. Competition among farmers (and, to a lesser extent, among irrigators and other users) for limited water was accompanied by the

---

[136]DEQ, "Water Quality Trading in NPDES Permits Internal Management Directive," Oregon Department of Environmental Quality Internal Management Directive (December 2009): www.deq.state.or.us/wq/pubs/imds/wqtrading.pdf. NPDES is the National Pollutant Discharge Elimination System.

[137]The COAG comprises the prime minister, state premiers, territory chief ministers, and the president of the Australian Local Government Association. The role of the COAG is to initiate, develop, and monitor the implementation of policy reforms that are of national significance and that require cooperative action by Australian governments.

perception that some potential new users placed higher marginal values on water than did existing users. This view was later supported by formal analysis.

The movement toward a nationally uniform system of tradable water rights began in 1994 with the adoption by the COAG of a strategic framework for reform of the Australian water industry.

Enabling Legislation. The COAG plan called for the institution of trading arrangements in water entitlements. In June 2004, COAG negotiations culminated in an agreement to establish a new national market to trade water rights, the National Water Initiative. The initiative marked a significant development in transboundary water regulation in Australia because it represented an acceptance of the incorporation of price and trading criteria into water management on a large scale.

In most Australian states, a licensing system now regulates water access and distribution. The licenses are often equated with water "ownership," but water in Australia remains a public good in legal terms. Licenses simply give the license holder the right to use an amount of water at a particular time and place.

Water trade in Australia involves trade in both water entitlements and seasonal water allocations. The difference is analogous to buying versus renting a home. One is viewed as temporary; the other, as permanent.

- Trade in water entitlements (sometimes referred to as "permanent trade") involves transferring the ongoing right to access water for the term of the entitlement. The two types of permanent entitlements are high security and general security. *High-security* entitlements receive allocations close to the full volume of entitlement, whereas *general-security* entitlements receive highly variable allocations of water ranging from 0% to 100%. High-security entitlements are valued far more highly than general-security entitlements.

- Trade in seasonal water allocations (sometimes called "temporary trade") involves transferring some or all of the water allocated to the entitlement to another party for the current irrigation season or an agreed number of seasons.

The water-trading program sets a cap on current water use and allows trading of current allocation licenses. Such trading enables new users to obtain water supply and allows current license holders who do not use their full allocations to sell excess water entitlements. In addition to providing a cap on water use, Australia's water-trading programs regulate different types of water use through the establishment of different water-access license types. Water licenses are given a priority rating, so in times of scarcity, those with less "secure" licenses are the first to lose entitlements and the permanent security license holders (such as drinking water providers and year-round irrigators—e.g., rice farmers) are protected. In New South Wales, for example, because rights are organized on a priority basis, if scarcity increases, the access entitlements are reduced, beginning with the lowest-priority license holders.[138]

States and territories have a legal responsibility to record water-access entitlement, ownership, and other trade details in a registry. As a result, regional variations can be found in registries in terms of information recorded, compatibility, and accessibility. The National Water Market System is undertaking work to improve efficiency, effectiveness, and compatibility of registers.

Entitlement-trading volume in 2011–2012 was 380 billion gallons (1,437 GL), and allocation trading was 1.1 trillion gallons (4,297 GL). In terms of market value, the overall turnover in Australia's water markets in 2011–2012 was estimated at $1.66 billion. This volume represents a 12% increase over the previous year.[139]

Case of the Murray–Darling Basin. The Murray–Darling Basin (which gets its name from the two major rivers in the basin, the Murray and the Darling) is by far the most active of the regional water-trading systems in Australia. It represents 70%–80% of all water traded in Australia (by volume). The basin is located in southeastern Australia and makes up the majority of Australia's prime agricultural land. The Murray–Darling Basin receives little rainfall; it gets most of its water for agricultural use from surface water. Nevertheless, the basin has a history of growing water-intensive crops, including cotton and rice, which are generally heavily irrigated.[140]

Prices for entitlements and allotments vary greatly, depending on geography, water availability, and other factors. The National Water Commission reports that water entitlements generally trade at higher prices than allotments. This case is intuitive because entitlements are permanent transfers and allotments are temporary. The prices of both entitlements and allotments appear to be driven also by basic supply-and-demand factors: Prices tend to be higher in areas where demand is greatest and water is scarce.

To demonstrate how price varies with geography, **Figure 6.1** provides entitlement prices for various geographical subdivisions of the Murray–Darling

---

[138]The source of this information and the report mentioned throughout this discussion is "Australian Water Markets Report 2011–2012," Australian Government National Water Commission.

[139]Because 1 GL is 810.7 acre-feet, in this example, entitlement trading is about 1,164,976 acre-feet and allocation trading is 3,483,578 acre-feet.

[140]A map of Australia showing areas discussed in this section is available at www.murrayriver.com.au/river-management/murray-darling-basin-commission.

Figure 6.1. Entitlement Prices across Water Systems in 2011–2012

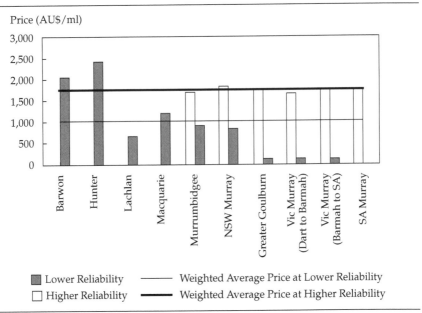

Notes: ml = milliliter. NSE = New South Wales. Vic Murray refers to the area of Victoria and the Murray River. Dart = Dartmouth. SA = South Australia.

Source: "Australian Water Markets Report 2011–2012," op cit.

water-trading system. As the figure shows, although a good bit of consistency characterizes high-reliability allotments, low-reliability allotments show a wide range of prices, depending on their location.

Figure 6.2 illustrates price variability across time in the various water systems within the Murray–Darling trading program. According to Figure 6.2, prices have declined drastically in all of the affected water systems. The National Water Commission reports that the lower prices are generally the result of increased rainfall in recent years relative to earlier years. Although these price declines follow a pattern similar to those in other markets, such as the SO2 market, it is probably too early to draw many parallels, particularly because the Murray–Darling markets seem to respond mainly to water availability. Nonetheless, these price declines are reminiscent of the price declines in the emissions markets.

Figure 6.3 shows permit prices for the Murrumbidgee high-security market in the Murray–Darling Basin. The Murrumbidgee is one of more than 15 separate active markets within the basin.

Effects of Water Trading in Australia. Water trading has many effects in Australia. In this section, we focus on one particular effect in the

Figure 6.2. Allocation Prices across Water Systems, 2008–2012

Source: "Australian Water Markets Report 2011–2012," op cit.

Figure 6.3. Quarterly Volume-Weighted Average Price for Murrumbidgee High-Security Market

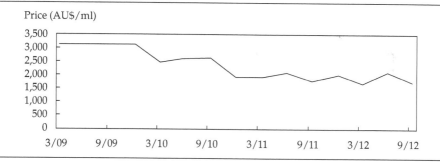

agriculture sector to illustrate the impact of water markets on agribusiness, investment, the environment, and—perhaps most importantly—the people participating in the market.

The implementation of the water market in the Murray–Darling Basin has brought about important changes in the way water is used there. Surveys conducted by the Australian Department of Agriculture, Fisheries and Forestry show that water trading is providing irrigated agribusinesses with an increased suite of options for optimizing water management on the farm. Some irrigators have reduced water use while others have expanded it, and those who reduce are able to sell water permits to those who expand.

Water trading has also allowed farmers to adjust their operations on the basis of water availability in a particular year. Research has shown that during a recent drought, some irrigators chose to actually reduce water consumption and sell water credits rather than attempt to further irrigate crops in such dry conditions. Additionally, water trading allows farmers who require fairly consistent levels of irrigation, such as those who grow tree-based crops, to purchase water credits from farmers who are able to adjust their crops on an annual basis. Surveys also show that water application rates went down in the 2006–10 period as farmers reacted to reduced water allocations by modifying their irrigation practices. As a result, the region has gradually seen a shift in production from low-water-value agricultural commodities to those of higher value, such as horticulture, vegetables, and fruit.

The Australian water market, one of the world's first large-scale experiments in water rights trading, has been successful in providing important price signals for market participants. Like other emissions rights markets, the Australian market incorporated important design steps. Its framers clearly identified and assigned the property rights, established clear limits for the use of the traded commodity, provided for transferability through a registry mechanism, and emphasized water management and monitoring. Other positive elements involve natural characteristics: Rainfall in Australia is highly variable, making water supply also quite variable; most of the water in the system can be traded from one zone to another, resulting in a more fungible commodity than within-zone trading only; and water can be held in reservoirs from one season to another, which makes supply adjustments possible. The Australian water authorities have also been active in the dissemination of economic research and data to market participants, important conditions for any successful market.

Technical Solutions to Water Scarcity

For Australia, trading in the rights to use water may have a positive impact on the supply of freshwater in the coming years. Future water demand estimates based on current projections of population and economic growth suggest that by 2030, water requirements will be 40% greater than current supply. One-third of the world's population, mostly in the developing world, will live in basins that have water deficits larger than 50%.

Solutions to water scarcity problems abound, but without knowing the true price of water, determining the *optimal* solution is difficult. Unfortunately, as a result of the lack of organized water markets, we are often left to guess which solution may be the best. Prices not only help inform us about which solutions are optimal but also encourage the development of the solutions themselves.

As seen in the SO2, CO_2, and other environmental markets, inventors of solutions are often driven by a market price. Command-and-control regulatory approaches to water scarcity, which is what we generally have in most countries today, are unable to provide the incentives found in markets. Although regulation and associated penalties are effective as sticks (i.e., punishment), they have a mixed record when it comes to carrots (i.e., reward). For this reason, we believe pricing and markets to be the better solution (pricing should apply only to the amount of water that exceeds the amount needed for health, hydration, and hygiene). For water markets to function properly, an effective regulatory regime must be in place to define property rights and to provide effective monitoring and enforcement. In the following sections, we discuss some of the technical solutions to water scarcity that exist today.

Water Infrastructure. Upgrading water infrastructure by fixing leaky pipes and valves represents one of the largest opportunities developed societies have to decrease water loss and, in effect, increase our water supply. Despite the fact that the United States is considered one of the global leaders in water infrastructure, the American Society of Civil Engineers reports that water leaks resulting from aging infrastructure cost the United States 2 trillion gallons and $3 billion annually. In the United States, up to 20% of water is lost to leaks. The estimate is that replacing the US water infrastructure would cost between $300 billion and $1 trillion. Unfortunately, water infrastructure investment in the United States and in most developed countries is chronically underfunded. Remedying this problem presents both significant challenges and significant investment opportunities. For-profit water management companies and public–private partnerships are likely to be key in bridging the gap in funding.

Among those companies working to fill the need for new and improved water infrastructure are Pentair (NYSE: PNR), which makes pumps, valves, and controls for the water industry; Mueller Water Products (NYSE: MWA), which focuses on water transmission and delivery; and Watts Water Technologies (NYSE: WTS), which focuses on valves and related products for the water industry.

Measurement, Monitoring, and Verification. An often-repeated saying is that what gets measured gets managed. Water is no exception. Unfortunately, little water gets measured and even less is properly managed. Much as increased energy efficiency often provides the best return on investment for companies and individuals hoping to reduce their energy bills, increased water efficiency through proper measurement and monitoring may be the most cost-efficient way to decrease exposure to water-supply risks. Proper water management requires intelligent instruments that allow for automated collection of information in real time. This information is necessary to make informed decisions about how to manage water resources. The information and decisions are important for investors and analysts, particularly in regions where water prices are on the rise and thus efficient use of water is most financially beneficial. In other words, as prices for water increase, the demand for measurement, monitoring, and verification products and services related to water use should also increase.

IBM (NYSE: IBM) is one of the companies at the forefront of water use monitoring, and it has provided positive results in pilot programs focusing on the implementation of water use–monitoring technology. In one case, real-time monitors providing water consumption data every 15 minutes were used in households in Dubuque, Iowa. The information was sent to the households to alert them to potential leaks and anomalies in water use. The city saw a decrease in water use of 6.6% during the pilot program, an amount projected to translate into 64.9 million gallons a year in savings.

Other companies working on water use monitoring and measurement include Pure Technologies (TSE: PUR), which provides monitoring and surveillance for physical water infrastructure, and TaKaDu, a private Israeli company that provides software to utilities for monitoring water networks.

Advances in Irrigation and Crop Science. Irrigation is one of the largest and most inefficient uses of water today. According to the US Department of the Interior, irrigation accounts for 34% of water demand in the United States. The UN estimates that 70% of all water withdrawals globally are for agriculture and expects this number to rise because of the increasing amount of land allocated to agriculture. Although many users of water, such as electric utilities and industrial users, return much of the water they take, irrigation water is almost never returned to its source. To make matters worse, more than half of all water used in irrigation is lost in the process of irrigating, either through evaporation or from leaks in irrigation systems. For these and other reasons, efficiencies in irrigation would represent a significant opportunity to save water, particularly in developing countries.

Much of the developing world continues to use flood irrigation, often losing nearly half of the water before it reaches the plant being irrigated. Micro and drip irrigation systems, bringing more than 90% of their water to the root zone of the plant, represent significant advances over flood irrigation. Even conventional sprinkler-based systems, which bring 50%–70% of their water to the root zone of the plant, are an improvement over flood irrigation. Among the companies providing advanced irrigation equipment are Toro Company

(NYSE: TTC), Jain Irrigation Systems in India (BOM: 500219), and John Deere (NYSE: DE).

Additionally, drought-tolerant seed varieties are likely to be in greater demand as rainfall levels decrease in some areas of the world. Many of the world's large crop-science companies provide seeds and other products to aid in drought tolerance; some are DuPont (NYSE: DD), Monsanto (NYSE: MON), and Syngenta AG (VX: SYNN).[141]

Water Treatment and Filtration. In 2008, Goldman Sachs estimated that the annual global sales of water- and wastewater-treatment products and services were $164 billion.[142] The type of treatment used for water depends on its desired end-use. Typically, water undergoes physical filtration processes that separate out the solids and is then treated chemically through disinfection or similar processes. Increasingly, residential water systems are being exposed to contaminants that were not on the radar when the water-treatment systems were designed and built. Runoff from agricultural operations, pharmaceutical by-products, and other household contaminants are driving a need for advanced cleanup technologies. Chemical treatment has been the preferred method of dealing with these contaminants, but new filtration and ultrafiltration methods are becoming common.

In addition to treatment methods, water conservation and recycling are playing increasingly important roles, particularly in the use of lightly treated wastewater for landscaping irrigation or to recharge groundwater aquifers.

Investment opportunities in water treatment and filtration include a wide variety of companies, such as Veolia Environnement in France (NYSE: VE), Sabesp in Brazil (NYSE: SBS), Aqua America (NYSE: WTR), Tianjin Capital Environmental Protection in China (SHA: 600874), and Severn Trent Water in the United Kingdom (LON: SVT).

Desalination. Given the scarcity of freshwater we have described, desalination systems have attracted a great deal of interest. Desalination is the removal of salt and other minerals from seawater. According to the International Desalination Association, more than 14,000 desalination plants were in operation worldwide as of 2009 and the market for desalination systems is experiencing growth of around 12% annually. These plants provide only a small amount of the global water supply but are particularly prevalent in the Middle East, where energy costs are relatively low and the water shortage is often acute.

Traditionally, desalination systems have been hindered by high energy requirements for producing potable water. Approximately 60% of the

---

[141]VX is the Six Swiss Exchange.
[142]Dray et al., "The Essentials of Investing in the Water Sector," op cit.

operation and maintenance cost for a desalination plant can be attributed to the cost of energy. The conventional treatment of surface water uses 0.2–0.4 kWh of energy per cubic meter (roughly 264 gallons) of water treated.[143] In comparison, desalination uses 2.6–3.7 kWh of energy.

Advances in the efficiency of desalination plants—in particular, in membrane technology—are beginning to make them cost competitive with more conventional sources of clean water. Currently, however, even with these efficiencies, the cost of desalination is prohibitive in much of the world. The Los Angeles County Economic Development Corporation estimates that over the life of the treatment facility, it costs at least $1,000 to treat each acre-foot of water.

With projected double-digit annual growth for desalination companies, however, many investors in recent years have found them an attractive investment. A difficulty facing average investors is that many of these companies receive only a fraction of their revenues from desalination activities. Such companies as Dow Chemical Company (NYSE: DOW), GE, ACCIONA in Spain (MC: ANA), Veolia Environnement, and Hyflux Ltd. (SI: HYFL) are leaders in desalination, although much of their revenues come from other business activities.[144] A few companies, however, do focus primarily, if not entirely, on desalination. IDE Technologies is a private Israeli company focused on desalination, and Consolidated Water (NASDAQ: CWCO) develops and operates desalination plants in the Caribbean.

An interesting aspect is that the cheapest water entitlements in the Australian market are priced at around $147/megaliter (ML) whereas one of the most efficient desalination plants in the world, located in Israel, produces freshwater at $510/ML (or 0.51 cents/kiloliter). Some economists believe that markets help drive down water prices and that trading may be cheaper than high-capital-expenditure water projects.

Related Investment Opportunities in Water

Investment opportunities related to water include equity investments, exchange-traded funds, and water funds and indices.

Water Equities. Opportunities in water stocks exist in filtration, infrastructure, desalination, engineering, treatment, testing, and other aspects of the water value chain. These areas can be broadly categorized into three groups: treatment, management, and infrastructure.

Many of the large banks and investment management firms publish lists of stocks that provide exposure to water, often broken down by market

---

[143]Leaving 10 100 watt light bulbs on for an hour consumes 1 kWh of energy.
[144]MC is the Barcelona Stock Exchange, and SI is the Singapore Stock Exchange.

segment. Many dozens, if not hundreds, of companies are available for investors to consider. Many of the world's largest companies—including GE, Dow, and United Technologies—are active in water. As noted, many of these large corporations receive only a small percentage of their revenues directly from water-related business. Among the large corporations that do receive a large percentage of their revenues from water are two French companies, Veolia Environnement and Suez Environnement (SEV: EN). Smaller companies that receive the majority of their revenues from water include Pentair, Kurita Water Industries (TYO: 6370), Aqua America, and Christ Water Technology (VI: CWTE).

Exchange-Traded Funds. ETFs have become increasingly popular with investors seeking exposure to a commodity or asset class that may otherwise be difficult to access. Water ETFs are no different in this regard. As interest in water-related investments has increased in recent years, so has the number of ETFs providing investors with exposure to the water market. Among these funds are the following:

- *The PowerShares Water Resources Portfolio* (PHO) is among the most popular water ETFs. All of the assets are based in the United States, and the fund focuses heavily on industrial water companies rather than utilities. It is made up primarily of mid- and small-cap companies that focus on water conservation and purification. Among the top holdings are American Water Works Company, Flowserve Corporation, and Toro Company.

- *The PowerShares Global Water Portfolio* (PIO) is split about 60/40 between industrial stocks and water utilities. Two of the larger holdings are Pentair and Flowserve. It is quite similar to PHO but is more global, although with significant allocations in the United States.

- *The S&P Global Water Index* is split evenly between water utilities and services, such as equipment and materials. It provides both US and international exposure.

- *The First Trust ISE Water Index Fund* is primarily a US equity ETF focusing on wastewater treatment and the potable water industry. Among the top holdings are Veolia Environnement and Mueller Water Products.

Water Funds and Indices. A handful of water-focused mutual funds have emerged in the past several years. Among the most popular are the following:

- *The Calvert Global Water Fund* holds about 100 companies focused on water utilities, water technologies, and water infrastructure. Most of its holdings are small- to mid-cap companies. The fund has total assets of more than $98 million and a three-year annualized return of +12.99%.

- *The Allianz RCM Global Water Fund* (AWTAX) invests primarily in companies in the S&P Global Water Index and the Palisades Water Index. It invests in companies involved with both water quality and water quantity. AWTAX holds 20–50 stocks. The fund has total assets of $126 million and a three-year return of +14.29%.

- *The Palisades Water Index* tracks the performance of companies involved in a wide range of activities along the water value chain. The sectors covered by the index include utilities, water treatment, analytical (e.g., water modeling, software), infrastructure, resource management, and multibusiness.

- *The Dow Jones U.S. Water Index* is composed of international and domestic companies that are affiliated with the water business. Companies are required to have a minimum market capitalization of $150 million.

- *The S&P 1500 Water Utilities Index* is a subset of the S&P Composite 1500 Utilities Index. It includes 50 companies that are in water-related businesses. The 50 companies are distributed equally between water utilities and infrastructure, on the one hand, and water equipment and materials, on the other hand.

Looking Ahead

Water is one of the few commodities on Earth we cannot live without. It is essential to our very existence and has a profound effect on the way we conduct our daily lives. From nourishment and sanitation to hygiene and commerce, water truly is the "drop of life." Given the scale of the water problems before us, ranging from agricultural runoff to aging infrastructure and a growing population, real changes are going to be required in the way we interact with and manage our water supply if we are to prosper as a species in the long run. If water is to become the most important commodity of the 21st century, as we predict, significant changes in the global water industry are both unavoidable and desirable. In this chapter, we discussed how these changes will provide opportunities as new markets, technologies, and policies develop to deal with the increasing demand and diminishing supply of freshwater. Investors able to understand the implications of these developments will be in a better position to profit from them than investors who turn a blind eye.

7. Weather Risks and Associated Asset Classes

On 29 October 2012, just northeast of Atlantic City, New Jersey, a hurricane named Sandy made landfall. "Superstorm Sandy," as it became known, delivered hurricane-force winds, widespread flooding, and storm surge (an increase in the sea level) across the Eastern Seaboard unlike anything that had been experienced since the Great New England Hurricane of 1938. As a result, insured losses—primarily in the United States but stretching from Jamaica to Canada and affecting most points in between—amounted to $30 billion; uninsured losses amounted to $35 billion. A total of 210 people lost their lives.[145] Unfortunately, Hurricane Sandy is part of a continuing trend toward greater and greater damages resulting from catastrophic events.

The trend toward greater damages is undeniable. Natural disasters—that is, hurricanes and earthquakes—appear to have been increasing globally in frequency over the last several decades. The dollar value of damages in the United States has been escalating particularly quickly because the US population has been migrating toward coastal regions, where the threat of natural disasters poses great risk. These demographic trends require that these areas provide new and improved infrastructure and require adaptations in commercial buildings, factories, and expensive dwellings. For these and other reasons, the value of insured property has soared. This trend has created a need for more capital in the insurance and reinsurance sectors. This chapter covers the major attempts to address these capital needs.

First, we discuss the establishment of new entrants into the market, the evolution of existing providers, and the emergence of Bermuda as a center for insurance and reinsurance. Second, we look at the development of catastrophe bonds. Third, we discuss the growth of industry loss warranties and swaps. Finally, we address the role of weather derivatives—catastrophe futures and options and heating- and cooling-degree day contracts.

Recent Natural Disasters and Insured and Uninsured Losses—in Brief

After some turbulent decades early in the 20th century, the 1970s were relatively quiet in terms of natural disasters. Most insurance and reinsurance companies covered their risk exposures internally. Until the late 1980s,

---

[145]Information in this section is from "Significant Natural Catastrophes 1980–2012," Munich Re NatCatSERVICE: www.munichre.com/app_pages/www/@res/pdf/NatCatService/significant_natural_catastrophes/2012/NatCatSERVICE_significant_eco_en.pdf.

insured losses for individual events typically did not exceed $1 billion. All these traits changed on 10 September 1989. Making landfall in the United States at Charleston, South Carolina, from Hurricane Hugo was a Category 4 hurricane that caused widespread damage, including 27 fatalities in South Carolina and 34 in the Caribbean.[146] Total economic losses are estimated to be $10 billion, with roughly half of that insured. Prior to Hugo, the largest insured loss from a hurricane had been from Hurricane Betsy in 1965, which produced insured losses of $2.3 billion, not adjusted for inflation.

Unfortunately, Hugo was only the beginning of the end for the relative calm that had characterized the insurance and reinsurance industries. Three years later, Hurricane Andrew hit southern Florida, Louisiana, and the Bahamas as a Category 4 hurricane, resulting in nearly $16 billion in insured damages. Prior to Hurricane Andrew, according to Property Claim Services, the cumulative insured damages from hurricanes in the United States since 1949 had been approximately $16.8 billion. Needless to say, Hurricane Andrew was a wake-up call to the insurance and reinsurance industry: Increased capital and diversification would be needed.

Table 7.1 shows that all 10 of the costliest natural catastrophes in history have occurred since 1990; 8 of the 10 have occurred within the last decade. Thus, a body of evidence indicates that the severity of natural disasters is on the rise. The financial impacts are clearly greater than at any other time in history, partly because of a rise in global population, a migration toward coastal areas, a rise in property values and the size and cost of homes, and a rise in the proportion of property that is insured. For example, each of what are now the three most populated states in the United States—California, Texas, and Florida—has seen a twofold to threefold increase in population since 1960, as shown in **Figure 7.1**. These are also coastal states with significant exposure to hurricanes, earthquakes, and drought.

Addressing the Need for Additional Capital

Attempts to fill the need for capital in the weather-related risk arena include new entrants into the reinsurance markets, catastrophe bonds, industry loss warranties, and swaps.

Entrants into the Insurance/Reinsurance Market and Establishment of Bermuda as a Market Center. It is somewhat ironic that the island after which the famed Bermuda Triangle is named is the home of a major risk mitigation center. Despite its dicey reputation, Bermuda is

---

[146]The Saffir–Simpson Hurricane Wind Scale rates each hurricane from 1 to 5 on the basis of its sustained wind speed. The scale thus estimates potential property damage. Hurricanes that are Category 3 and higher are considered severe.

Table 7.1. Ten Costliest Events Worldwide, 1980–2011
(ordered by insured losses in original dollars)

Period	Event	Affected Area	Overall Losses	Insured Losses	Fatalities
25–30 Aug 2005	Hurricane Katrina, storm surge	US: New Orleans, Slidell (Louisiana); Biloxi, Pascagoula, Waveland, Gulfport (Mississippi)	$125,000	$62,200	1,322
11 Mar 2011	Earthquake, tsunami	Japan: Honshu, Aomori, Tohoku; Miyagi, Sendai; Fukushima, Mito; Ibaraki; Tochigi; Utsunomiya	210,000	40,000	15,840
24–31 Oct 2012	Hurricane Sandy, storm surge	Bahamas, Cuba, Dominican Republic, Haiti, Jamaica, Puerto Rico, US, Canada	65,000	30,000	210
6–14 Sep 2008	Hurricane Ike	US, Cuba, Haiti, Dominican Republic, Turks and Caicos Islands, Bahamas	38,000	18,500	170
23–27 Aug 1992	Hurricane Andrew	US: Homestead (Florida); Louisiana; Bahamas	26,500	17,000	62
15–18 Nov 2011	Floods	Thailand: Phichit, Nakhon Sawan, Phra Nakhon Si Ayutthaya, Pathum Thani, Nonthaburi, Bangkok	43,000	16,000	813
Jun–Sep 2012	Drought, heat wave	US: Midwest	20,000	15,000–17,000	100
17 Jan 1994	Earthquake	US: Northridge, Los Angeles, San Fernando Valley, Ventura, Orange (California)	44,000	15,300	61
7–21 Sep 2004	Hurricane Ivan	US, Caribbean, Venezuela, Colombia, Mexico	23,000	13,800	120
22 Feb 2011	Earthquake	New Zealand: South Island, Canterbury, Christchurch, Lyttelton	16,000	13,000	185

Source: Geo Risks Research, Munich Re NatCatSERVICE: www.munichre.com/en/reinsurance/business/non-life/georisks/natcatservice/default.aspx.

Figure 7.1. Population Growth in Selected US States, 1960–2010

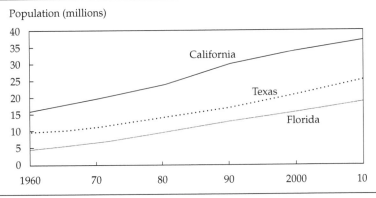

Note: The latest census was taken in 2010.

Source: US Census Bureau.

home to more than half of the major global reinsurance companies and is a global hub of the insurance industry. Many of the industry's thought leaders live and work there. As of 2012, Bermuda is home to 1,400 insurance companies, with total assets of $442 billion.[147] The primary reason is Bermuda's favorable tax structure: Bermuda has no tax on corporate profits. Also, Bermuda has a relatively stable political and economic environment.

In reinsurance, primary insurers pass on some of the risk they incur from writing homeowner or auto policies to another insurer, the reinsurer. Reinsurers sometimes then pass on or "retrocede" this risk to additional reinsurers in an effort to further spread risk. Thus, reinsurance offers insurance companies a way to spread risk, provide financing, and increase the amount of coverage they can provide.

In the early 1960s, "captive" insurance companies—those owned by large companies to insure their employees—began to establish themselves in Bermuda. As the number of captives grew, Bermuda began to build infrastructure that allowed the insurance industry to grow. The Insurance Act 1978 was passed, and the Insurance Advisory Committee, a group of insurance companies that advise the government of Bermuda on matters related to the industry, was formed.

When Hurricanes Hugo and Andrew awoke the insurance and reinsurance industries from their multidecade lull, new companies were created to address the need for additional capital. This realignment as the *re*insurance industry resulted in the emergence of numerous Bermuda-based companies, beginning

[147]Greg Wojciechowski, "ILS Flock to the BSX," *Bermuda Reinsurance Magazine* (Spring 2012): www.bermudareinsurancemagazine.com/article/ils-flock-to-the-bsx. Accessed 4 June 2013. ILS is insurance-linked securities.

with Mid Ocean Reinsurance (a private company) in 1992. Prior to this time, no reinsurance companies specialized in property catastrophe reinsurance.

However, although additional capital was injected into the industry through the reinsurance companies, the industry clearly needed to move to nontraditional sources of financing for additional risk capital. One such source was catastrophe (or "cat") bonds. As these new financing instruments evolved, dedicated cat funds appeared.

As of May 2013, the total volume of insurance-linked listings, which includes cat bonds and reinsurance-linked investment funds, on the Bermuda Stock Exchange (BSX) exceeded $7.06 billion.[148] The BSX is the world's largest offshore and fully electronic exchange offering listings and trading opportunities for international and domestic issuers of equity, debt, depositary receipts, insurance securitization, and derivative warrants.

Catastrophe Bonds. A cat bond is a fixed-income instrument in which the payment of the coupon or the return of the principal of the bond—or both—is linked to the occurrence of a specified catastrophic event. Cat bonds have become the primary way of spreading insured catastrophe risk to the capital markets. The issuers, or sponsors, typically include insurance and reinsurance companies, corporations, and government agencies, and the investors are generally large institutional investors, hedge funds, pension funds, bond funds, and other insurance and reinsurance companies.

The basic economic logic of cat bonds is as follows: An insurance company wants to hedge the risk that it will have to pay large claims in case of, say, a hurricane. The insurance company offers investors a well-above-average yield if a hurricane does not occur but reduces or eliminates payments to investors if the catastrophe does occur; if the catastrophe occurs, the company, instead, uses the money to help pay claims. The expected return to investors, probability weighted across catastrophe and noncatastrophe scenarios, is high enough to compensate investors for the risk taken; meanwhile, the insurance company has eliminated some of its operating risk without having to contract with a reinsurer.

Cat bonds emerged in the 1990s in response to the large-scale economic effects of several US hurricanes, including Hurricane Andrew. The bonds are rated by ratings agencies and sold through investment banks in much the way that traditional bonds are rated and sold. Cat bonds are created as special-purpose vehicles (SPVs) and are usually domiciled in Bermuda or the Cayman Islands. The SPV has a reinsurance agreement with the sponsor. Investors

---

[148]Artemis, "Over $7 Billion ILS and Cat Bonds Listed on Bermuda Stock Exchange for First Time," *Artemis* (21 May 2013): www.artemis.bm/blog/2013/05/21/over-7-billion-ils-and-cat-bonds-listed-on-bermuda-stock-exchange-for-first-time/.

purchase the bonds through primary issuances. The proceeds from the bond sales are deposited into a trust account, and the sponsor deposits a premium payment to the trust account. The proceeds from the bond sale and the premium from the sponsor are typically invested in US Treasury money market accounts. Quarterly, the investors are paid interest from the money invested and a portion of the premium in the form of coupons. If the event characterized in the cat bond prospectus occurs, the SPV releases the collateral held in the trust account owned by the SPV to the sponsor.

Because capital markets have such a large capacity for absorbing risk, cat bonds have become a useful tool for insurers to diversify their capital base to include entities other than those that may already have a portfolio concentrated on catastrophe risk, such as reinsurers. Additionally, in the years after the global financial crisis, capital market participants and managers of institutional capital pools viewed cat bonds as a diversifying asset class because the gains and losses are not directly tied to those of conventional asset classes. The diversification benefits of including cat bonds in investment portfolios have been supported by a number of notable studies. Cummins and Weiss (2009),[149] for example, measured the correlation between the investment performance of cat bonds and that of various bond instruments and indices. The results for the period preceding the global financial crisis (January 2002–June 2007) show almost no correlation between cat bond returns and the return of the other investments.

Cat bonds are often viewed as inherently risky, however, in part because of their binary nature. Their payoffs are usually tied to either an indemnity trigger, index trigger, or parametric trigger (see the section "Industry Loss Warranties"). An *indemnity trigger* is the actual loss incurred by the insurer after an event has taken place in a prespecified geographical region and line of business—for example, an Illinois snowstorm with damages in excess of $20 million between 1 January 2013 and 1 January 2014. If the catastrophe for which the bond was written occurs, the buyer may lose its entire investment. Although the likelihood of that particular catastrophe occurring is remote, the downside is clearly substantial. If the catastrophe does not occur, then the insurance company pays the buyer the full coupon and principal of the bond.

The first cat bond was issued in 1995. Several cat bonds were issued in 1996 and 1997 involving sponsors and underwriters from the United States and other countries. They covered numerous types of perils, including earthquake, wind, hail, aviation, marine, and other disasters and ranged over a wide geography.

---

[149]J. David Cummins and Mary A. Weiss, "Convergence of Insurance and Financial Markets: Hybrid and Securitised Risk-Transfer Solutions," *Journal of Risk and Insurance*, vol. 76, no. 3 (September 2009):493–545.

Cat bond issuance has grown steadily since the bonds' inception in 1995. Some analysts would note, however, that in light of the size of the insured losses in recent years, the amount covered by cat bonds is still small. **Figure 7.2** shows the growth in issuance over time and a breakdown by type of issuance in the past 10 years.

Cat bonds have the advantage of being able to replicate a traditional reinsurance contract. This trait has played a role in the popularity of cat bonds with insurance companies. The inherent flexibility of cat bonds also means that they can be tailored to fit the bond issuers' specific needs. Additionally, because cat bonds are fully collateralized from inception, unlike most traditional reinsurance agreements, the issuers and investors can mitigate counterparty credit risk.

In part as a result of increased investor demand, cat bond spreads, representing the extra return the insurer pays investors to take on the risk, have decreased significantly as of the time of this writing.

Industry Loss Warranties. Unlike traditional insurance or reinsurance policies, which pay the insured for any realized losses, an industry loss warranty (ILW) typically pays off on the basis of the total losses that an event causes the *entire insurance industry* to suffer. Alternatively, an ILW may pay off on the basis of an event parameter, such as an earthquake in the city of

Figure 7.2. Catastrophe Bond Issuance by Type of Risk

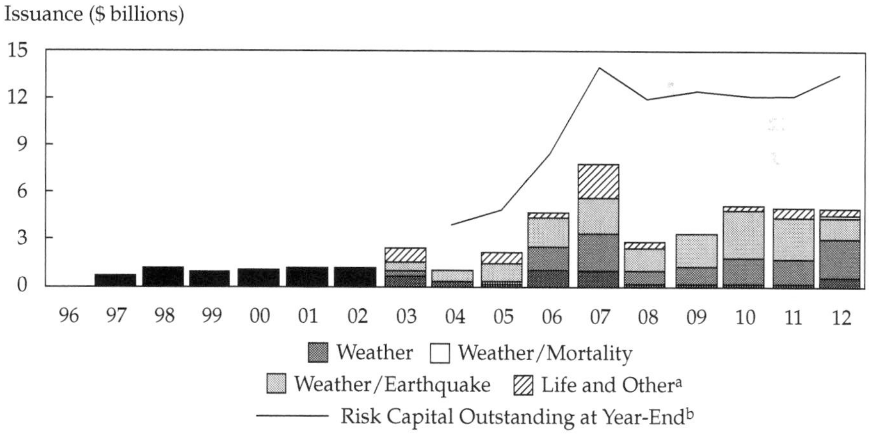

[a]Life and Other includes mortality, peril, life, and worldwide risks.
[b]The values for 2012 are partial year.

Notes: Data before 2003 are not broken down by type.

Sources: Sebastian von Dahlen and Goetz von Peter, "Natural Catastrophes and Global Reinsurance—Exploring the Linkages," *BIS Quarterly Review* (December 2012): www.bis.org/publ/qtrpdf/r_qt1212e.htm. Data from Artemis and Guy Carpenter.

San Francisco with a magnitude of 7.0 or above on the Richter scale, which would trigger the policy payment. Neither of these structures is familiar (because most insurance pays the insured for losses specific to that party), and would-be investors in ILWs need to carefully study the specific ILW contract before considering an investment. In the San Francisco earthquake scenario, for example, the ILW would simply state that the payment of a $200,000 premium results in $10 million in coverage. The $10 million is paid if a previously approved verifier reports that an earthquake of 7.0 or higher magnitude has occurred in the predetermined geographical area.

ILWs, like cap bonds, are a way the capital markets have created to assume some of the catastrophe risk of the reinsurance industry. A distinguishing feature of ILWs is the use of an *industry loss index* or *parametric index* as a trigger for the payout.[150] The industry loss index most commonly used in the United States is calculated by Property Claim Services (PCS). PCS industry loss estimates are based on a survey of industry representatives, such as insurers and emergency managers. Other indices or datasets used are Munich Re NatCatSERVICE, Carvill Hurricane Index, PERILS, and Swiss Re Sigma.[151] Unlike the industry loss trigger, parametric triggers are based on the physical characteristics of a catastrophic event, such as the San Francisco example given previously. Because parametric triggers are not based on insured losses, however, the insured may not receive the precise loss amount resulting from the catastrophic event.[152] Note that some cat bonds are also triggered by combined industry losses and catastrophe parameters.

A classic ILW takes the form of a bilateral reinsurance contract. Index products are available, however, that take the form of derivatives or exchange-traded instruments.

ILWs have been in existence since the 1980s and have gained traction as a result of their relative simplicity. Because payouts are triggered by an index that tracks losses to all the insurers with exposure to a given potential catastrophe, ILWs allow the investor to focus on the quality of the index rather than conducting due diligence on the underwriting criteria of a particular insurer. This feature allows ILWs to be easily standardized. The downside of this standardization is the basis risk associated with the instrument; that is, ILWs do not often correlate well with the potential losses of the insurer and can, therefore, be seen as less desirable when compared with such alternatives as catastrophe bonds.

---

[150]ILWs may also feature a dual trigger that includes more than one parameter (i.e., wind speed plus a minimum level of losses to the insured).

[151]de Burca, "Industry Loss Warranties: The Basics" (August 2011): www.jdsupra.com/documents/9eae29ba-0204-46d3-86b9-711cea275007.pdf. Accessed 3 June 2013.

[152]RMS, "Cat Bonds Demystified: RMS Guide to the Asset Class," Risk Management Solutions (2012): https://support.rms.com/Publications/Cat_Bonds_Demystified.pdf. Accessed 4 June 2013.

Although there is no centralized database for pricing and volume of ILWs, some reinsurance companies and researchers publish estimates. **Figure 7.3** presents estimates for ILW capacity and premiums (the reinsurance premium divided by the reinsurance limit is known as the rate on line [ROL]). As Figure 7.3 shows, the ILW market was nearing record highs for both premium cost and volume of business in 2012.

Catastrophe Insurance Futures and Options. Cat bonds and ILWs are generally traded over-the-counter (OTC).

The first futures contracts on catastrophe insurance were launched by the Chicago Board of Trade (CBOT) in 1992. The basis of these futures was an index tracking the losses of about 25 property and casualty insurers, which reported their loss data quarterly to the Insurance Services Office, a firm that provides data on property/casualty insurance risk. As the first futures contract designed to mitigate risks other than price and interest rate risk, catastrophe futures were considered too novel at the time and were not met with enthusiasm by insurance companies. The CBOT eventually changed this futures contract from a loss ratio to a simpler cash option, which had the advantage of resembling an insurance contract. At the height of its success, catastrophe options had an open interest of 20,000 contracts. The options contract eventually floundered, however, and was delisted in 1999. Since then, other

Figure 7.3.   ILW Capacity and Premiums

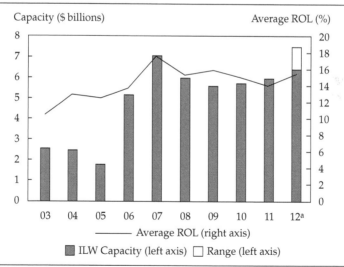

aInitial estimate.

Source: Willis Re, "Q1 2012 ILW Update" (January 2012): www.willisre.com/documents/Media_Room/Publication/Willis_Re_Q1_2012_ILW.pdf.

exchanges—including the Insurance Futures Exchange, the Chicago Mercantile Exchange (CME), and the Eurex Exchange—have introduced varieties of catastrophe derivatives. None of these products received significant traction, however, as a result of such factors as basis risk, the lack of a continuous information flow that is needed to support trading, and lack of efforts to educate investors and market the products.

Swaps. Another way of spreading catastrophe risk to the capital markets is through swaps. Broadly speaking, a swap is the exchange of the cash flows from one security for those of another. A swap allows an insurer to gain exposure to an investor's portfolio of returns while the investor gains exposure to the revenues associated with the premiums received by the insurer. Each party provides a series of periodic payments to the other. The insurer's payments are based on a portfolio of the investor's securities; the investor's payments are based on potential catastrophic losses predicted by an industry loss index.

Two insurers can also engage in a swap. For example, Swiss Re can exchange part of its North Atlantic hurricane and European windstorm risks for Mitsui Sumitomo Insurance Co.'s Japanese typhoon exposure.[153] These are high-risk events for both companies, and by swapping segments of it, both insurance companies can diversify their risks.

Weather Derivatives. Weather derivatives provide another way to hedge the risks associated with natural disasters or even more mundane weather events, such as erratic rain and snowfall patterns. They are especially important because, according to US Department of Commerce figures, more than a third of total US economic growth is linked to weather conditions.

Weather derivatives began to be traded in the mid-1990s, a time when energy and utility companies in the United States started to deregulate. The increased competition created an incentive for these companies to hedge their risk exposures to stabilize their earnings. Because weather conditions had a very tangible impact on energy demand, OTC weather deals between these companies started to emerge. Not until 1999, however, did the CME begin listing futures and options on temperature indices of 10 US cities.[154] In 1998, the global weather derivatives market was estimated to be a $500 million

---

[153]J. David Cummins, "CAT Bonds and Other Risk-Linked Securities: State of the Market and Recent Developments," *Risk Management and Insurance Review*, vol. 11, no. 1 (2008):23–47 (http://homepage.univie.ac.at/franz.diboky/RI2/CAT_Bonds.pdf).

[154]Melanie Cao, Anlong Li, and Jason Wei, "Weather Derivatives: A New Class of Financial Instruments," working paper (January 2004): www.yorku.ca/mcao/cao_wei_weather_CIR.pdf. Accessed 4 June 2013.

industry.[155] By 2011, this market had grown to $12 billion.[156] In the following section, we describe some of the most common weather derivatives today and their practical applications.

▩ *Heating-degree and cooling-degree days.* A heating-degree day (HDD) measures the amount of energy required to heat a building. Specifically, an HDD is the number of degrees that a day's average temperature is below 65° Fahrenheit (in the United States), the temperature below which buildings generally need to be heated. A cooling-degree day (CDD) does the reverse by measuring the number of degrees that a day's average temperature is above 65° Fahrenheit, when people typically start to use air conditioning to cool their buildings. Given the increasing fluctuations in temperature over the years—a phenomenon commonly attributed to climate change—it is not surprising that exchanges have created weather derivatives to hedge these risks.

The CME has two such contracts listed: the US Seasonal Strip Weather HDD and the US Seasonal Strip Weather CDD futures and options. The prices of the HDD and CDD futures are based on the CME Degree Days Index, which tracks the total number of HDDs and CDDs in a month. The settlement prices of the futures and options are calculated by summing up these HDD and CDD values for a month and then multiplying them by $20. These instruments can help entities with weather risk exposure—such as farms, resorts, and utilities—manage their exposures to fluctuating temperature.

▩ *Other weather derivatives.* Although utilities constitute the majority of the end-users of HDD/CDD contracts, many other businesses have revenues that are tied to the weather. Examples are insurance companies, agricultural firms, and even ski resorts. Weather-related risks for agriculture may include rainfall levels, hurricanes, wind, and hail, whereas ski resorts may be concerned about a lack of snow. Weather derivatives exist for each of these risks, but they are not all traded as standardized contracts on an exchange as HDD and CDD contracts are traded. They trade OTC.

Weather-Related Investable Indices. In recent years, banks have introduced a growing number of products intended to encourage a broad range of investors to bet on the effects of a changing climate—namely, the impact of carbon emissions and rising global temperatures. In 2007, UBS launched a Global Warming Index, and in the following year, it launched the world's first integrated tradable investment benchmark that tracks the greenhouse effect, the Greenhouse Index. The Greenhouse Index comprises a combination of weather

---

[155]J. Finnegan, "Weather or Not to Hedge," *Financial Engineering News*, no. 44 (2005).

[156]*Resilience: Winning with Risk*, Special Focus on Global Risks, no. 3 (2013): www.pwc.com/en_GX/gx/governance-risk-compliance-consulting-services/resilience/issue3/assets/pwc-harnessing-financial-innovation.pdf. Accessed 4 June 2013.

(CME HDD and CDD futures) and emissions asset classes (European Union Allowances and Certified Emission Reductions futures traded, respectively, on the IntercontinentalExchange and Nord Pool Spot) and allows market players to gain exposure to greenhouse gas emissions and their impact on the weather. For example, the level of the index rises as the prices of carbon emission credits and global temperatures rise. Both retail and institutional investors can go long or short the UBS Greenhouse Index and the Global Warming Index in the same way they can the S&P 500 Index.[157]

Weather Funds. A number of specific weather funds are currently investing in the derivatives market. An example is the Cumulus Energy Fund of City Financial in the United Kingdom. By concentrating on specific weather events important to energy trading—such as temperature, snowfall, rainfall, and wind—the hedge fund is able to provide investors with risk exposures they may not find in more traditional funds.[158] Another example is the Nimbus Fund, a $2.5 billion–plus fund based in Bermuda and run by Nephila that invests in weather derivatives and catastrophe risk insurance.[159]

Looking Ahead

In 2011, the United Nations estimated that natural disasters would cost the world a record amount—more than $380 billion in that year alone. According to a report by Swiss Re, total economic damage from disasters—naturally occurring or otherwise—is estimated to have been at least $140 billion in 2012. Hurricane Sandy alone was estimated to have inflicted $30 billion to $50 billion worth of damages, making it the second most expensive storm in US history (after Hurricane Katrina, with $125 billion).

In 2011, the size of the policyholder surplus (capital reserves) of the US insurance and reinsurance industries to insure all of the property and casualty risk of a $15.6 trillion economy was $550.3 billion for insurance and $108 billion for reinsurance. A single catastrophic event striking major wealth centers, such as California, Florida, Texas, or New York, could have wiped out the entire capital of the US insurance and reinsurance sectors. Had Hurricane Katrina hit New Orleans more directly, the consequences would have been significantly worse. Therefore, clearly, opportunities abound for weather-related and insurance-linked securities to help shift some of these risks from insurance and reinsurance companies to the wider capital markets.

---

[157]UBS 2007 environmental report: www.ubs.com/global/en/about_ubs/corporate_ responsibility/commitment_strategy/reporting_assurance/reports.html.

[158]See the City Financial website. Cumulus Funds are described at www.cityfinancial.co.uk/ node/420.

[159]Nephila is described at www.nephila.com/.

8. Sustainability and Associated Asset Classes

The focus of previous chapters has been on emissions markets, use rights, and other environmental derivatives as asset classes. Then, we discussed investment opportunities associated with these individual asset classes. We took a bottom-up view of environmental finance. The primary focus of this chapter is a top-down view of portfolio investments that are termed "sustainable."

Sustainability investing (SI), or socially responsible investing (SRI) as it is often referred to in the United States, denotes any investment strategy that seeks to consider environmental and social considerations as well as financial return. Sustainability, viewed as an investment philosophy, has led to the development of an asset class of portfolio investments (typically, stocks and bonds) that are consistent with this philosophy. We focus specifically on portfolios of equities that reflect environmental criteria. We do not provide an exhaustive view but, rather, an overview of this important and growing investment strategy.

Since 1996, assets managed under the banner of SI have grown from $166 billion to more than $3 trillion in the United States alone—a 19% compound annual growth rate.[160] Externalities, particularly environmental externalities, are gradually being reflected in equity investments. This trend is complemented by a management emphasis on sustainability and by increased transparency in corporate environmental disclosures. The undeveloped "social stock exchanges," which connect social projects and businesses with investors, that now exist could evolve to provide a marketplace for sustainable investment financial asset classes. In addition, a breed of investment popularly called "impact investment" is emerging that ties investment returns to actual social and environmental performance criteria. Investors must learn to navigate this new investment landscape and adapt accordingly.

Overview of Sustainability Investing

Prior to the mid-1990s, the use of environmental and social criteria in investment decision making consisted almost entirely of SRI screens. These screens identify sectors in which investors choose not to invest—that is, companies or industries that are engaged in activities the investor deems harmful to society. Ethical investing was popularized during the Vietnam War with the establishment of the Pax World Fund, the first socially screened mutual fund. It

---

[160]The "2012 Report on Sustainable and Responsible Investing Trends in the United States" can be found at www.ussif.org/trends.

offered an alternative investment option to those opposed to weapons production. This movement became globalized in the 1970s through the Sullivan Principles, which underpinned an international effort to end apartheid in South Africa.[161]

As SI evolved, it began to use not only values-driven negative screens but also positive investment choices designed to encourage environmentally friendly business practices and maximize financial return in a socially responsible framework. Another significant development between early and modern forms of SI was the growth of shareholder activism. In the 2000s, academics and investors began to place increasing emphasis on the importance of good corporate governance in a company's risk-and-return profile, a trend partially driven by the Sarbanes–Oxley Act of 2002.

As SI evolved, so did analysts' ability to screen companies on the basis of environmental and social criteria. Early practitioners operated primarily as niche players, but many of today's largest institutional investors use sustainability principles.

Just as corporations are adopting sustainable business practices to increase their "triple bottom line" (or positive impact on shareholders, other human stakeholders, and the natural environment), investors are pushing for greater integration of sustainability principles in their investment analyses.[162] The object is to *increase* their financial returns, not sacrifice financial return to pursue other goals. The result has been the promulgation of numerous environmental, social, and governance (ESG) measures in the mainstream investment market.[163]

Specifically, prescient investors have started to incorporate climate change and other environmental risks into their investment analyses to maximize financial return and reduce financial risks. Climate change is among the most important issues in today's sustainability universe. The physical risks of climate change—be they hurricanes, earthquakes, rising sea levels, or changes

---

[161]The Sullivan Principles were formed by the African-American preacher Rev. Leon Sullivan. They later grew in popularity among US corporations. New global Sullivan Principles were established by Rev. Sullivan and UN Secretary General Kofi Annan in 1999. They advocated the expansion of corporate social responsibility in all that concerns human rights and social justice regardless of national boundaries.

[162]The phrase "triple bottom line" was first coined in 1994 by John Elkington, who founded a British consultancy called SustainAbility. He argued that companies should be preparing three bottom lines: profit, people (a measure of how socially responsible the corporation is), and planet (a measure of how environmentally friendly it is).

[163]ESG denotes the three central factors used in measuring the sustainability and ethical impact of an investment in a company or business. Within these three areas are a broad set of concerns that are increasingly being included in the nonfinancial factors that figure in the valuation of equity, real estate, corporations, and fixed-income investments of all types. ESG is the catchall term for the criteria used in SRI.

in the amount and location of arable land—together with political and regulatory shifts make it crucial for investors to factor climate change into their investment strategies.

Risks are not the only reason for SI. Exciting new opportunities await investors as sustainability becomes increasingly important. In particular, sustainability is emerging as a key driver of innovation among existing corporations and startups. Rich investment opportunities are possible in the industries where innovations flourish, such as the clean technology sector.

Size and Key Drivers of the SI Market

In 2012, the US SIF Foundation identified $3.74 trillion worth of assets that are either managed under ESG guidelines or held by investors who filed or co-filed shareholder resolutions on ESG issues at publicly traded companies.[164] The US SIF Foundation started measuring the size of the US sustainable investing market in 1995. By 2012, the assets in this space had increased by 486%. **Table 8.1** shows the growth in this period.

According to the US SIF Foundation 2012 report, the recent growth of SI has been driven by several factors:[165]

- The growing realization in the investment community that climate change and resource scarcity have tangible impacts on financial returns.

---

[164]US SIF—formerly the Social Investment Forum—is the US membership association for professionals, firms, institutions, and organizations engaged in sustainable and responsible investing: http://ussif.org/.

[165]The "2012 Report on Sustainable and Responsible Investing Trends in the United States" can be found at www.ussif.org/trends.

Table 8.1. Sustainable and Responsible Investing in the United States, 1995–2012 ($ billions)

	1995	1997	1999	2001	2003	2005	2007	2010	2012
ESG	$166	$533	$1,502	$2,018	$2,157	$1,704	$2,123	$2,554	$3,314
Shareholder resolutions	473	736	922	897	448	703	739	1,497	1,536
Overlapping assets	—	−84	−265	−592	−441	−117	−151	−981	−1,106
Total	$639	$1,185	$2,159	$2,323	$2,164	$2,290	$2,711	$3,069	$3,744

Notes: "Overlapping assets" involved in some combination of ESG incorporation (including community investing) and shareholder advocacy are subtracted to avoid potential double-counting. Separate tracking of the overlapping strategies began only in 1997, so no data are available for 1995. Prior to 2010, assets subject to ESG incorporation were limited to socially and environmentally screened assets.

Source: US SIF Foundation.

- Increasing demand from institutional and individual investors, together with the mission and values of their management firms. These factors are putting pressure on investment managers to incorporate ESG factors into their investment analysis and portfolio construction. According to the US SIF 2012 survey, client demand and values were motivations cited by 72% of managers.

- The emergence of sustainability accounting standards. According to Trucost, an independent environmental research agency, annual "external" environmental costs (i.e., costs that do not appear on corporate financial statements) for 800 companies in 11 industry sectors rose from $566 billion in 2002 to $846 billion in 2010.[166] Accordingly, the Sustainability Accounting Standards Board (SASB) was launched in 2012. This board established voluntary industry-specific sustainability accounting standards for use in 10-K and 20-F forms. These actions caused sustainability to become an issue for chief financial officers. It complements the Financial Accounting Standards Board, which developed the accounting principles currently used in US financial reporting.

- Sustainability's increasing adoption by corporate top managers as a means to grow profits and gain competitive advantage. Walmart's chief executive officer, for example, hosts biannual meetings on sustainable practices for his leadership team. At one of the recent meetings, a report noted that Walmart now earns $230 million annually through its waste-management program.

- From 2010 to 2012, increased support by voters of corporate proxies on environmental and social resolutions. In that period, 30% of environmental and social issues resolutions won support, whereas the rate was 15%–18% in 2007–2009.

Building a Sustainability Portfolio

Investors have many ways to invest in a portfolio of equities with a sustainability approach. Examples include portfolios that have been screened for ESG and independently tailored to investors, green mutual funds, and investable indices for corporate sustainability.

Following the 2008 financial crisis and the establishment of the SASB in 2011, focus on integrated reporting that combines financial and sustainability information has sharpened. Sustainability reporting involves measuring, disclosing, and being accountable to internal and external stakeholders for organizational performance in progress toward sustainable business practices.

---

[166]These data should be taken as indicative rather than absolute.

"Sustainability reporting" is a broad term considered synonymous with triple bottom line, corporate responsibility reporting, and other terms that are used to describe reporting on economic, environmental, and social impacts.

The most common way to assess a company's environmental risks and sustainability measures is to evaluate the company's corporate social responsibility (CSR) report. CSR reports provide information (primarily on an annual basis) on a company's performance as it relates to environmental, social, and governance criteria. A typical CSR report includes information on a company's human resources, management, and corporate governance (diversity, career training, health and safety, etc.); environmental impact (emissions, water use, waste processing and reuse, plant safety, etc.); and social awareness (community programs, sensitivity training and awareness, etc.). Companies may also set internal targets for these measures and report that performance. Although CSR scoring and internal goals may reveal ESG profiles, analysts are encouraged to look at other aspects of a company's actions to evaluate its social and environmental performance.

In the past, corporations set and followed their own standards and reporting formats in publishing CSR information. In recent years, however, efforts have begun to standardize the reporting criteria and the measurement and reporting formats. The Global Reporting Initiative (GRI) has developed voluntary standardized reporting and measurement criteria that make corporate sustainability reporting much like financial reporting. With a framework for sustainability reporting and the benefit of standardization, the GRI allows the creation of comparable and credible reports among organizations.[167] The SASB, an independent body outside the financial regulatory system, also aims to create new standards for companies in the system.

In addition to individual corporate reporting and disclosures, several organizations have taken the lead in the analysis and ranking of corporate performance with respect to sustainability and environmental accountability. Notable examples are the Carbon Disclosure Project and CERES. Although each organization has its own unique method, the general approach is similar—a survey questionnaire to gauge companies' sustainability attributes and rank them accordingly.

These organizations exemplify the clear trend toward an increased appetite for standardized measurement and increased transparency. In addition to evaluating general environmental risks, a growing number of customized analytical tools have been designed to evaluate specific environmental risks, such as those associated with water and energy sources.

---

[167]The standardization process for sustainable criteria is in its initial stage. The number of social and environmental screening criteria and industry-specific criteria makes this process complex. Standards cannot be assumed to be scientific or statistically valid.

Sustainability-Focused Mutual Funds

Sustainability approaches are making growing inroads into the management of mutual funds. One of the earliest mutual funds in this field was the Calvert Social Investment Fund (CSIF), established in 1982, which divested (refused to invest in) certain stocks to protest apartheid in South Africa. In 1986, CSIF became the first fund to sponsor a socially responsible shareholder resolution.

Sustainability-driven funds can focus on large-, medium-, or small-cap companies. Like other mutual funds, sustainability-focused mutual funds serve both individual and institutional investors, may involve several investment strategies, and usually invest in fixed-income or equity securities. **Table 8.2** provides a sampling of sustainability-focused mutual funds.

Commonly, these funds have a special ESG focus. For example, the CRA Qualified Investment Fund invests in fixed-income securities that support community development activities, such as affordable housing, environmental initiatives, and small-business development. A different approach is taken by the Neuberger Berman Socially Responsive Fund, which screens for companies that demonstrate leadership in the environment, workplace practices, community relations, supply chain sustainability, and product integrity. Some mutual funds also screen for companies' records in public health and the nature of their products; for example, they might actively avoid investing in companies that produce alcohol, tobacco, and military weapons, which are goods and services perceived to have especially undesired externalities.

Table 8.2.   A Sampling of Sustainability-Focused Mutual Funds

Fund Category/Name	Ticker
Large-cap equity	
Vanguard FTSE Social Index Fund	VFTSX
Neuberger Berman Socially Responsive Fund	NBSRX
Parnassus Equity Income Fund	PRBLX
Small- to mid-cap equity	
Parnassus Small-Cap Fund	PARSX
Equity specialty	
TIAA-CREF Social Choice Equity Premier	TRPSX
International equity	
Gabelli SRI Green Fund	SRIAX
Praxis International Index Fund	MPLAX
Balanced equity and fixed income	
PAX World Balanced Fund	PAXWX
Fixed income	
CRA Qualified Investment Fund	CRAIX

The largest sustainability-focused mutual fund today, by assets under management, is the Parnassus Equity Income Fund. With close to $6 billion in assets, although it is still significantly smaller than the top mutual funds, it is one of the best-performing funds based on average 10-year return.

Other examples of sustainability-focused mutual funds today are Guinness Atkinson Alternative Energy and Firsthand Alternative Energy, both of which invest primarily in equity securities of companies that are involved in alternative energy or the energy technology sectors.

As of 2012, some 333 mutual fund products in the United States considered environmental, social, or corporate governance in their holdings. They had total assets of $640.5 billion. In contrast, only 55 SRI funds were available in 1995, with $12 billion in assets. The Forum for Sustainable and Responsible Investment regularly updates a comprehensive database of all US-based green mutual funds and makes this information available to the public.[168]

Sustainability Equity Indices

In addition to sustainability-focused mutual funds, sustainability-focused equity indexing has emerged. Sustainability indices measure the financial performance of companies that meet various ESG criteria. These indices can be a proxy for the impact that sustainable practices have on shareholder value and, therefore, serve as key reference points for company managers and investors. In this respect, sustainable indices perform a function similar to that of such equity indices as the S&P 500 or the Dow Jones Industrial Average.

Two drivers led to the conception of indices for sustainability investment in the mid-1990s. First, investors recognized that corporate sustainability has a positive impact on long-term shareholder value. Second, investors became increasingly comfortable with the idea that environmental risks and the impact of sustainable practices can be measured and quantified.

Recently, the concept of sustainability indices has evolved to include other areas in environmental finance. Not only are there indices for specific environmental sectors, such as solar energy, but there are also indices for newly commoditized environmental assets, such as carbon allowances.[169]

Generally, sustainability indices are constructed from the stock prices of companies that satisfy certain sustainability criteria. Such an index is the earliest form of sustainability index and probably the most common. Notable indices in this category are the Dow Jones Sustainability Indices (DJSI).

---

[168]Information about the Forum for Sustainable and Responsible Investment may be found at http://charts.ussif.org/mfpc/.

[169]The World Federation of Exchanges provides an exhaustive list of sustainability indices: http://www.world-exchanges.org/sustainability/WFE-ESG.pdf.

The first sustainability index was the Dow Jones Sustainability World Index (DJSI World), designed by Sustainable Asset Management and Dow Jones in 1999. Today, the DJSI family is used by investors around the world to manage sustainability-driven portfolios and used by companies to evaluate their sustainability performance. In fact, a growing number of companies have defined inclusion in a sustainability index as one of their corporate goals. Not only is this trend a robust indicator of the growing importance of corporate sustainability in the business community, but it also demonstrates the business community's heightened awareness that companies' environmental and social strategies are linked to their market and financial strategies.

The methodology for calculating, reviewing, and publishing the DJSI mirrors that of the Dow Jones Global Indices. Using the 2,500 largest companies in the Dow Jones Global Total Stock Market Index as the starting universe, the DJSI World selects the top 10% of companies in terms of sustainability in each sector—that is, the companies considered the "best in class." This selection is based on a systematic corporate sustainability assessment.

As for public companies, their sustainability strategies are becoming more integrated with the companies' core businesses, as evidenced by a surge of companies that are publishing sustainability reports together with their usual financial reports. In addition, external verification and internal assurance systems are becoming more prevalent.

Recently, a number of equity indices have been created with exposures to specific environmental risks in mind, such as those associated with air pollutants or water scarcity. For example, FTSE has developed an index that provides carbon-risk-adjusted versions of the general FTSE index. The constituent companies are the same as those in the FTSE, but their weights have been changed on the basis of their exposure to carbon risk relative to their sector peers. This adjustment helps investors incorporate specific environmental risks into their overall investment strategies. Similarly, the S&P Global Water Index provides liquid and tradable exposure to 50 companies from around the world that are involved in water-related businesses.

Some indices focus on a specific sector, such as the WilderHill New Energy Global Innovation Index, which comprises companies worldwide that specialize in development technologies and services that focus on the generation and use of clean energy. Another example is the Deutsche Börse DAXglobal Alternative Energy Index (Bloomberg: DXAEP), which consists of companies that generate more than 50% of their revenues from alternative energy, such as natural gas, solar, wind, and hydro. Subcategories may also include geographical subindices, such as the DJSI North America.

Conclusion

Clearly, from this discussion of customized portfolios, sustainability-focused mutual funds and indices, and sustainability as an investment philosophy, the asset class of sustainability-focused investments is a growing field. Sustainability-focused investing has even percolated into emerging economies, such as China and India, which are now leaning toward transparent and standardized disclosures of companies' environmental activities. Given this continuing trend in the United States and abroad, sustainability promises to be an important asset class in the future.

9. Conclusion: You *Can* Put a Price on Nature

Wealth creation in the United States has changed dramatically since 1970. After World War II, from 1945 to 1970, wealth creation in the United States was largely driven by manufacturing. US manufacturing strength helped the country lead the world in value creation, as indicated by gross domestic product growth during that period: In terms of real (inflation-adjusted) chained 2005 dollars, GDP went from $2.22 trillion in 1945 to $4.70 trillion in 1970.[170]

The decade of the 1970s was different. Inflation was high, and commodity prices rose sharply. Furthermore, the 1973 Arab oil embargo, a bad wheat crop in the Soviet Union, and crop failure in the United States caused wheat and oil prices to explode upward. The combination of these factors meant that wealth creation in the 1970s was driven by commodities and other sectors that benefited from inflation. Agricultural concerns, energy companies, and storied commodity traders were the major wealth creators of the decade.

This situation changed again in the 1980s with the arrival of financial reforms in the banking and savings-and-loan community and a multitude of financial innovations. In that decade came the full development of the financial futures markets, where interest rates and money are commoditized. This phenomenon was punctuated with the creation of interest rate swaps. The commoditization of corporate debt via high-yield bonds led to further wealth creation. These so-called junk bonds enabled entrepreneurs who could not access the traditional capital markets to finance their ventures. Junk bonds financed, to name only a few, the first cable company and the cell phone. Such bonds also made leveraged buyouts possible, enabling inefficient companies to be taken over and reformed by new owners.

The drivers of wealth creation changed again in the 1990s. This decade was driven by innovations in technology. Great fortunes were made in personal computers, telecommunications, and software. The birth of the internet was heralded by the rise of Cisco Systems, Netscape, Yahoo, and, somewhat later, Google. This trend continued with such social networks as Facebook and such communication media as Twitter. All of these developments are enabling the commoditization of data, communications, and information. What is next?

The past shows that wealth creation is guided by fundamental structural and technological changes in the economy. This lesson from history leads

---

[170]"US Real GDP by Year" (www.multpl.com/us-gdp-inflation-adjusted/table).

us to believe that the next macro trend will be the commoditization of air and water. Environmental and economic shifts, policy changes, technology improvements, and other innovations will trigger this transformation. Population growth, the rise of China and India combined with their rising incomes and energy demand, resource scarcity, and a warming planet will fundamentally affect the economic fabric of tomorrow's world.

The world population is expected to reach 10 billion by 2050, which will increase stress on the environment. Demands for food and energy are all expected to increase manifold, driving demand for water. Water is the oil of the 21st century. Consider: China's per capita water resources are a quarter of the global average, and 8 of its 28 provinces are as dry as the Middle East. Water shortages cost China 2.3% of its GDP a year.[171] India is not far behind. As the world continues to warm, extreme weather events appear to be on the rise.

An economic shift is also taking place in the world. China and India, where most of the world's population resides, are rapidly lifting their populations out of poverty. Within a generation, the middle class in China has the potential to be roughly four times the size of the US middle-class population. By 2030, China should have approximately 1.4 billion middle-class consumers. India's middle class should number 1 billion in fewer than 20 years.[172] With higher incomes and standards of living comes higher demand for better-quality products, and an increasing standard of living includes a demand for better environmental quality. Governments and corporations around the world will be compelled to tackle this issue. As we have shown throughout this book, stewardship of the environment is moving out of the realm of philanthropic activity and is becoming an important business and public policy issue.

Technological advances will also provide a stimulus for this transition. The transformation is already being shaped by disruptive technology innovations in clean energy systems, environmental applications with "big data" (datasets so large and complex that they are hard to process with traditional

---

[171]According to a 2009 World Bank report, "Addressing China's Water Scarcity," of that 2.3%, 1.3 percentage points are attributable to the scarcity of water and 1 percentage point to the direct impact of water pollution. This estimate is likely to be below the true total cost, however, because it does not include the cost of effects for which estimates are unavailable. These effects may include the ecological impacts associated with the drying up of lakes and rivers and the amenity loss from the extensive pollution in most of China's water bodies. The report can be found at www-wds.worldbank.org/external/default/WDSContentServer/WDSP/IB/2009/01/14/000333037_20090114011126/Rendered/PDF/471110PUB0CHA0 101OFFICIAL0USE0ONLY1.pdf.

[172]Kenneth Rapoza, "Within a Generation, China Middle Class Four Times Larger Than America's," *Forbes* (5 September 2011).

data-processing applications), clean transportation, and building construction innovations.[173] Wind power is already reaching cost parity with conventional electric power generation in some regions, and solar energy is trending in the same direction. Some 70% of the new global power generation capacity added between 2012 and 2030 is projected to be from renewable technologies. We are also witnessing improvements in energy efficiency in a variety of applications. Such technological innovations as smart grids, batteries, and storage devices provide efficiencies on the demand side of electricity.

We are also witnessing policy shifts. Past successful experiences with using market mechanisms to tackle environmental issues are spurring greater experimentation with these economic tools. Closely supporting this effort are financial and banking sector reforms, particularly in previously closed economies. For example, national exchanges have opened and trading in commodity derivative instruments has begun in many parts of the world, including India and China. Although still in their infancy, these changes will assist in defining property rights, standardizing and commoditizing new environmental products, and, most importantly, providing price discovery and transparency. All of these factors will combine to provide the structural change required for the transition to a greener economic pathway for global growth.

This book has introduced the reader to the birth of a new asset class—the environment. The commoditization of environmental assets has the potential to be the principal driver of wealth creation in the near future, and this shift has already begun. In fact, as discussed, the environment is not the commodity of the future but *today's* commodity.

The commoditization of sulfur dioxide helped in the effective management of acid rain in the United States. Similarly, carbon dioxide allowances are helping the world cope with climate change. Weather has been commoditized in an effort to deal with catastrophic events, and weather-related futures and options markets and fixed-income securities have come into being. The increased concern for the environment has also affected the equity markets. Sustainable indices and portfolios have been created. They capitalize on investors' and portfolio managers' needs to deal with environmental, social, and governance challenges.

Our emphasis throughout this book has been on pricing various negative externalities and establishing rights of use. If property rights in public goods are established and transaction costs are minimized, prices can guide the private and public sectors toward achieving environmental and social objectives at the lowest cost to society. The cap-and-trade model and emissions trading

---

[173]A "disruptive innovation" is an innovation that helps create a new market and value network and, eventually, disrupts an existing market and value network (over a few years or decades), displacing earlier technology.

were used to illustrate the benefits of using market-based mechanisms and economic tools for managing environmental problems.

Successful cap-and-trade programs in combating air pollution all followed 12 simple steps—the "clean dozen."

The Clean Dozen

1. Define the commodity—the right to emit a unit of a pollutant, called an "allowance."

2. Define clear and unambiguous property rights. Provide a legal infrastructure to ensure that the owner of a commodity has a clear title to it.

3. Determine the covered emitters in air pollution programs.

4. Establish a baseline—the level from which to reduce the pollution level.

5. Establish a reduction schedule for the pollutant.

6. Establish a registry that initializes ownership of allowances and facilitates their transfer.

7. Using the registry, allocate those rights to the covered emitters in accordance with the reduction schedule.

8. Monitor and verify the pollutants produced by the covered emitters.

9. Define compliance so that if emissions by the emitters are equal to the emissions rights in the account, the covered emitters are in compliance. This step allows emitters to purchase or sell emissions rights to be in compliance.

10. Create periodic auctions to facilitate price discovery and transparency.

11. Facilitate over-the-counter spot and forward markets in addition to organized exchanges.

12. Enable futures and options to be issued and traded so that covered emitters can cost-effectively minimize current and future risk.

Examples of successful markets that used the clean dozen are SO2 allowances to combat acid rain in the United States, renewable energy certificates in New Jersey to stimulate the development of solar power, CO_2 allowances in the European Union Emissions Trading Scheme (EU ETS) to combat global warming, water rights in Australia to combat drought, and fishing rights in Alaska to prevent overfishing.

Lessons Learned

In addition to the clean dozen, a number of lessons are to be learned by policymakers and investors from the successful programs.

1. Keep It Simple. The message from past programs is that the perfect should not be the enemy of the good. Keep it simple. The programs provided private incentives to reach specific environmental objectives. Importantly, their goal was captured in legislation and a regulatory framework that was clear and unambiguous. More regulation did not necessarily mean better regulation. The goal was to reduce pollution, not punish the polluter. The program participants knew what the regulation entailed, who the regulator was, and the consequences of not reaching the target. These objectives were all captured in legislation and regulation that enabled the growth of the market. Collectively, the results of the programs demonstrate that the paradigm could be changed from profiting from polluting to profiting from *not* polluting.

2. Simple Does Not Mean Easy. Simply stating the goal is only the first step. Past successful programs facilitated building institutions that led to minimization of transaction costs in achieving the objectives. They also created the technological infrastructure needed to operate the programs successfully. Infrastructure included stack emissions monitoring to monitor SO2 emissions in the Acid Rain Program and electronic registry systems in that program, the EU ETS, and other programs. Building these programs involved the training and use of huge numbers of human resources in the form of emissions verifiers, accountants, lawyers, traders, and so forth. History teaches us that a combination of software (in the form of human and governance structures) and hardware (in the form of technological and legal enforcement infrastructure) are required for successful execution.

3. It Is All about Price. Price can teach us three important lessons: It can change behavior; a low price does not imply failure; and policymakers should focus on the program's design and results, not on its price.

■ *Price changes behavior.* Once a resource is priced fairly, its use is optimized. Optimization helps the program reach the environmental objective in the most cost-effective way. In the past, forecasters underestimated the role of price in changing behavior and promoting innovation. As the Acid Rain Program, the EU ETS, and other programs have proved, forecasters use the cost of pollution control of existing or known technology as the basis for emissions-rights pricing. They are consistently wrong. Price forces individuals and corporations to optimize and use resources judiciously. Thus, this mechanism triggered shifts to lower-pollution fuels and efficiency improvements.

It also triggered better accounting for energy use and environmental impact. Price signals also spur innovation in technologies and free up resources. History has taught us that it is generally a bad idea to sell short humanity's ability to invent and adapt. Policymakers and investors are wise to be guided by the experience that these emissions-trading programs provide.

▪ *Low price does not mean failure.* The price of an emissions allowance is not an indicator of the success or failure of the program. Achieving the environmental goal is. Price formation is merely a function of the reduction target: If high prices in rice and wheat result in an abundance of food, we cheer. With regard to pollution rights, however, we recognize that this commodity is different from food because the scarcity of such rights is created by government regulation. Shrill voices of criticism from people of varying political persuasions were heard when prices to emit fell below the marginal costs of abatement. In the Acid Rain Program, the criticism abounded for more than a decade yet significant reductions occurred, precisely because of the flexibility of cap-and-trade. Fuel switching was responsible, and it demonstrates the power of the price signal. The same was true in the EU ETS.

▪ *Leave the price alone.* The price is merely an output of the program design and drivers. Attempts to "fix" the program must focus not on making the price rise but on modifying the underlying fundamental design. For example, the low prices in the EU ETS right now can be remedied by making the environmental goals more ambitious instead of artificially manipulating the price. When changing reduction targets is not politically feasible, other policy tools, such as price floors, have emerged (as happened in California).

4. Policy Can Make or Break a Program. Many of the markets described in this book function on a stage built by government policy. Legislation creates these markets and drives environmental outcomes. Similarly, uncertainties in environmental policy and regulation often spell the demise of the program. Both the Acid Rain Program and the EU ETS were threatened by this phenomenon.

5. Flawed Market Architecture Hinders Success. Faulty design can result in damages to the program and losses for investors. Renewable identification numbers in the market for transportation fuels are the perfect example. The lack of a registry, violating a basic principle (Rule 6) of the clean dozen, resulted in the creation of counterfeit certificates. Policymakers and investors should always be wary of these design flaws. They are often caused by a lack of institutional memory as a result of changes in elected officials. Alternatively, they may arise when the design of a new program is assigned to branches of government that lack experience in creating markets.

Food for Thought and Major Trends

The history of environmental markets, lessons learned, and structural shifts shaping tomorrow's world present us with many opportunities.

The shale revolution is already transforming the US energy landscape. New technology in the form of hydraulic fracking and horizontal drilling have made it cost-effective to unearth natural gas and oil assets in shale that could make the United States the largest producer of energy in the world. Cheap natural gas is affecting all aspects of the economy, from manufacturing to power generation to transportation. What would be the implications if cheap natural gas were made available, either through domestic production or imports, to the rest of the world, particularly Asia and Europe? Shale can fundamentally change energy and, therefore, the environmental equation in the world.

What does cheaper natural gas mean for renewable energy and its competitiveness in the energy mix? Many environmentalists argue that the shale revolution could spell doom for the renewable energy industry. History has taught us that technology and innovation can be major economy shifters. Can advances in renewable energy technology enable it to be a competitive alternative to cheap fossil fuel? At the micro level, solar power continues to be a promising form of renewable energy. Developments in energy storage may drive further opportunities in wind and transportation. Biofuels may offer additional opportunities in renewable energy. Smart electrical grids may also provide investment opportunities. Price has the potential to spur energy efficiency, but because of the current structure of how we pay for electricity (after the fact, not as we consume it), electricity prices do not have the impact on conservation that they could have.

Transportation is the elephant in the room when you consider emissions, energy efficiency, and other topics we have discussed in this book. Transportation currently requires a highly concentrated, lightweight energy source that can be safely used in a vehicle. Hydrocarbon fuels fit the bill. To date, externalities from transportation have not been addressed by any program in a coherent fashion. Imagine what price signals and incentives could achieve in the transportation sector—electric cars, aviation (although this sector is currently being addressed by the EU), and biofuels!

The major trends that we see are as follows:

1. *Water will be the biggest commodity of the 21st century.* Perhaps the biggest problem and, therefore, the biggest opportunities lie in water. Desertification is possibly a more immediate problem than climate change. Only three continents have a better-than-adequate supply of water—North America, South America, and Europe. Water trading exists by dint of the

grain trade, but it is insufficient to meet the demands in Africa, India, and China or, for that matter, to avert regional shortages in the United States and Canada. The quantity of freshwater is only one part of the equation. Water quality is the second part. The success of water markets in Australia and Pennsylvania suggests that markets can address shortages of water quantity and quality. Pricing should create incentives to develop infrastructure, generate conservation (the equivalent of energy efficiency in carbon markets), and foster innovation. In related developments, investors should be watching for opportunities in transporting water efficiently and economically and in setting standards for water use in the hydraulic fracturing (fracking) process. Such standardization is the first step in facilitating the limitation of pollution caused by fracking.

2. *Environmental markets will continue to grow.* The environmental marketplace is vibrant with activity around the world. Contrary to the notion that the world will have a unified environmental market, we are witnessing a "plurilateral" system that includes regional, state, and national markets.[174] In the United States, California is leading the way. California has been an agent of change for more than a century—in film, high tech, social media, and the environment. California is already forging alliances with other carbon markets that are developing nationally and internationally. Policymakers and investors should follow the trends in California closely. In the United States, environmental solutions tend to begin at the state level and then percolate to the federal level.

Whereas the developed world shies away from market solutions to environmental problems, emerging economies do not. China, with seven separate cap-and-trade markets, is leading the way. China's policies started by focusing on promoting energy efficiency (as defined in Chapter 5), and the programs are morphing into cap-and-trade markets. India also has an energy efficiency–trading program. Cap-and-trade markets are under consideration in Brazil, South Korea, Mexico, Vietnam, and Kazakhstan. In assessing the future of cap-and-trade, investors may be better served by closely watching Sacramento, California, and Beijing than by watching Washington, DC, or Brussels. Emerging markets that begin developing environmental policies by setting energy-efficiency goals are on the right track, and investors should look at countries that adopt such goals as indicators that cap-and-trade markets are likely to develop.

---

[174]*Plurilateral* refers to the development of a framework for GHG emissions trading involving a medium-sized set of countries (e.g., 5–20). The concept of a plurilateral regime was coined by Richard L. Sandor in the mid-1990s. Although it was first published in 1999, it was not fully defined until 2001 in the following publication: Richard Sandor, "The Case for Plurilateral Environmental Markets," *Environmental Finance* (September 2001).

3. *The costs of catastrophic events will rise.* Eight of the top ten most expensive weather events have occurred since 2003, and those that affected the United States cost the US economy billions of dollars in losses. We expect this trend to continue and intensify, with further increases in insured and uninsured losses. This trend has huge implications for the financial industry as a whole. Management of such catastrophes can change the nature of the private insurance industry as well as government emergency assistance and self-insurance. Does the insurance industry or government have sufficient capital to cover the extent of future catastrophic losses? In addition, the impact of major earthquakes on nuclear power generation is all too clear. The Fukushima nuclear disaster triggered shutdowns in nuclear power plants around the world. What is the effect of such shutdowns on building new nuclear capacity, particularly in India and China, where power demand is growing fastest?

As demonstrated throughout this book, markets in emissions and user rights have solved environmental problems and created enormous investment opportunities. They achieved these ends by commoditizing the externality and then pricing it. The same concept has been applied to weather-driven events and catastrophes. The convergence of the environment and finance is here to stay, and the market mechanisms described in this book are only the beginning. The new asset class of environmental goods is just in its infancy and holds enormous promise.

Finally, we note that financial innovation and markets have a significant role to play in other situations and fields where there are good and bad externalities, such as medicine, education, and biodiversity. The best is yet to come.

Appendix A. Cap-and-Trade

Suppose that two emissions sources each emit 100 tons during a baseline period (a reference situation used to define emission reductions). If the policy mandate is to reduce overall emissions by 20%, one means of achieving that goal would be to assign each of the two emitters 80 tons of tradable emission allowances (for a total of 160 tons). Each emitter would then be required to monitor and report (using prescribed methods) its emissions and to annually achieve compliance by surrendering to the program authority emission allowances in an amount equal to its year-long emissions. **Figure A.1** illustrates the essence of such a cap-and-trade emissions-trading system.

Although each emitter has a nominal reduction target of 80 tons (20 tons below its baseline), the emitter represented by the middle bar in Figure A.1 was able to cut its emission to 40 tons, giving it a surplus of 40 emission allowances that it could sell to the other emissions source (or, in many programs, could bank for possible use or sale in later periods). The emitter represented by the bar on the right did not reduce its emissions; in fact, its emissions rose to 120 tons. Because it must surrender to the program authority emission allowances representing 120 tons of emissions, it must acquire 40 tons of emission allowances from other emitters who have made extra emission reductions. In this simple case, one emitter has just enough surplus allowances to sell to the

Figure A.1. Cap-and-Trade Emissions-Trading System

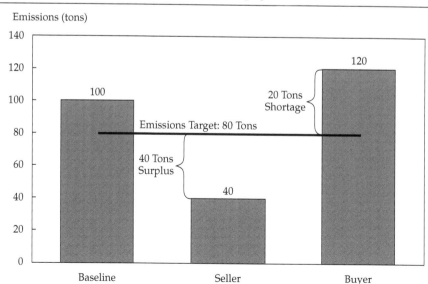

emitter that experienced rising emissions. Together, the two emitters reduce total emissions to the desired amount, which is 160 tons (40 + 120).

Suppose an emitter projects that its emissions will increase during the year—as a result of increased demand for its product or service, lack of low-cost emission-reduction opportunities, or perhaps the need to meet other regulatory mandates—and it finds it cannot easily purchase surplus emission allowances from others. In that case, it may bid up the price of emission allowances to induce others to sell to it. If this emitter fails to acquire allowances, it will have to weigh the choice among curtailing production, taking high-cost measures to reduce emissions while maintaining production, or in many programs, pay a fine (and possibly still be required to acquire and retire emission allowances at a later date).

Cap-and-trade is a cheaper alternative to a command-and-control system. Suppose there are two plants, Plant A and Plant B, that contribute to air pollution. An engineering analysis finds that Plant A has options to upgrade its equipment, install emissions-control devices, switch fuels, or take other managerial actions that could allow it to reduce air emissions by several tons at a cost of \$0.50 per ton reduced. A similar analysis for Plant B finds that its cheapest option will cost \$2.00 per ton of reduced emissions.

Figure A.2 illustrates the costs of emission. Suppose a new environmental regulation requires the owners of Plant A and Plant B to take actions that

Figure A.2.   Cost of Emission Reductions

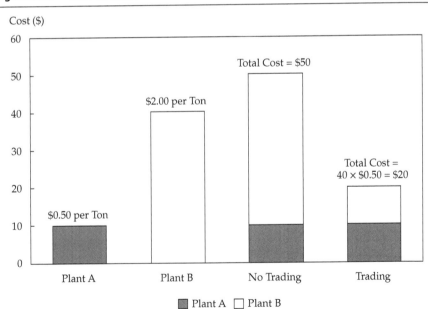

reduce *overall* air emissions by a total of 40 tons. The third and fourth vertical bars illustrate the total cost society would face to achieve the 40 tons of emission reductions with and without the flexibility allowed through emissions trading. If emissions trading were not allowed, Plant A would have to reduce its emissions by 20 tons (at a cost of $10) and Plant B would have to reduce its emissions by 20 tons (at a cost of $40). The total mitigation cost faced by society in this case would be $50. If emissions trading were allowed, Plant A and Plant B could both find an economically superior outcome by negotiating to have the low-cost Plant A reduce emissions by 40 tons and allow Plant B to meet its obligations of cutting its emissions by 20 tons by hiring—through an emissions trade—Plant A to make the extra cut on its behalf. Plant A could sell its environmental protection service—in the form of a tradable emissions credit—to Plant B, which could then present the credit to the environmental regulator as evidence that Plant B met its commitment to make sure 1 ton of acceptable emission reductions was realized.

As long as Plant A is willing to sell emission-reduction credits to Plant B at less than $2.00 per ton, then (in the absence of transaction costs), Plant B spends less money complying with the regulation by buying credits instead of cutting its own emissions. (Naturally, the environmental regulator would have to enforce all rules that might affect local air quality in the vicinity of Plant B. For this example, we assume the pollutant has no particular health impact on those close to the source, in the way that nitrogen oxide emissions from transport do.)

The total cost to society is $20 in the trading scenario (Plant A spent a total of 40 × $0.50 = $20 to cut its emissions by 40 tons). The amount paid by Plant B to Plant A is a cost to one side but a revenue to the other, resulting in no extra net cost to society.

Appendix B. Standardizing Greenhouse Gas Emissions

The Kyoto Protocol seeks to limit emissions of six greenhouse gases implicated in global warming:

1. Carbon dioxide (CO_2)

2. Methane (CH_4)

3. Nitrous oxide (N_2O)

4. Sulfur hexafluoride (SF_6)

5. Hydrofluorocarbons (HFCs)

6. Perfluorocarbons (PFCs)

Each of these gases contributes differently to overall global warming. Scientists measure the relative differences in global warming potency by using global warming potential (GWP). The GWP of a gas refers to how much heat it is able to trap over a standard period of time relative to carbon dioxide. The international measure for the time period is 100 years, and the reference gas, CO_2, has a GWP of 1. For example, the GWP for methane is 21, which means that methane emissions are 21 times more potent than CO_2 over a 100-year period in terms of trapping atmospheric heat. From an emissions-accounting standpoint, emitting 1 ton of methane is equivalent to emitting 21 tons of carbon dioxide. This equality is commonly considered "carbon dioxide equivalent" or CO_2e and bears a 1:1 relationship with the GWP.

The GWP of all greenhouse gases and the equivalent quantity of emissions in CO_2e terms are given in **Table B.1.**

Table B.1. Greenhouse Gases' GWP and CO_2e

Gas	GWP	CO_2e (tons)
Methane	21	21
Nitrous oxide	310	310
Sulfur hexafluoride	23,900	23,900
Hydrofluorocarbons	140–11,700	140–11,700
Perfluorocarbons	9,200–23,900	9,200–23,900

Source: Intergovernmental Panel on Climate Change, "IPCC 4th Assessment Report Climate Change 2007" (www.ipcc.ch/publications_and_data/ar4/wg1/en/ch2s2-10-2.html).

From a trading standpoint, the unit of account for emission credits or GHG emission allowances–trading programs around the world is usually 1 ton of CO_2e. Hence, in the methane example, emitting 1 ton of methane would require 25 CO_2e emission allowances to offset it. If this offset was done on 26 February 2013 using European Union Allowances (EUAs) based on market-determined prices (and closing EUA prices for the March 2013 EUA futures contract from the IntercontinentalExchange), then it would cost (25 EUA × €4.30/EUA) = €107.50.

Named Endowments

The Research Foundation of CFA Institute acknowledges with sincere gratitude the generous contributions of the Named Endowment participants listed below.

Gifts of at least US$100,000 qualify donors for membership in the Named Endowment category, which recognizes in perpetuity the commitment toward unbiased, practitioner-oriented, relevant research that these firms and individuals have expressed through their generous support of the Research Foundation of CFA Institute.

Senior Research Fellows

Financial Services Analyst Association

For more on upcoming Research Foundation
publications and webcasts, please visit
www.cfainstitute.org/learning/foundation/.

Research Foundation monographs
are online at www.cfapubs.org.

Made in the USA
Lexington, KY
30 November 2014